I0070844

Cybersecurity for Everyday Users: A Practical Guide to a Safer Digital Life

E. Psaila

Cybersecurity for Everyday Users: A Practical Guide to a Safer Digital Life

Copyright © 2025 by E. Psaila. All rights reserved.

First Edition: **February 2025**

No part of this publication may be reproduced, distributed, or transmitted in any form or by any means, including photocopying, recording, or other electronic or mechanical methods, without the prior written permission of the publisher, except in the case of brief quotations embodied in critical reviews and certain other non-commercial uses permitted by copyright law.

ISBN: 978-1-923432-36-9

Table of Contents

Chapter 1: Introduction: The Digital World and Why Cybersecurity Matters

In today's interconnected world, digital technology underpins nearly every aspect of our personal and professional lives. From the way we communicate to how we shop, work, and even manage our health, the digital landscape offers remarkable convenience and opportunities. However, as our dependency on technology increases, so too does our vulnerability to cyber threats. This chapter lays the foundation for understanding the modern digital world, the risks that come with it, and how this guide will empower you to safeguard your online life.

1.1 The Evolving Digital Landscape

1.1.1 A Journey Through Technological Advancements

Over the past few decades, technology has undergone a dramatic transformation. What began as simple communication via emails and basic websites has evolved into a complex network of interconnected devices and systems. Key milestones in this evolution include:

- **The Rise of the Internet:** The early days of the internet revolutionized how we access information, transforming libraries and encyclopedias into instantaneous digital repositories.

- **Mobile Revolution:** The advent of smartphones and tablets put computing power in the palm of our hands, enabling constant connectivity regardless of location.

- **Cloud Computing:** With data storage and processing moving to the cloud, individuals and businesses alike enjoy unprecedented flexibility and scalability.

- **Internet of Things (IoT):** Everyday devices—from refrigerators to thermostats—are now "smart" and connected, creating a seamless digital ecosystem but also expanding the attack surface for cybercriminals.

1.1.2 The Benefits and Challenges of a Connected World

The digital era has ushered in a host of benefits:

- **Efficiency and Productivity:** Automation and real-time data access have streamlined business processes and personal tasks.

- **Enhanced Communication:** Social media, video conferencing, and instant messaging have brought people closer than ever before.

- **Innovation and Convenience:** Technological advancements have led to innovative services, such as online banking, telemedicine, and e-commerce, making everyday life more convenient.

However, with these benefits come significant challenges:

- **Increased Exposure to Threats:** As more personal data is shared and stored online, cybercriminals have a larger pool of targets.

- **Complexity of Systems:** Modern networks and devices are intricate, making them harder to secure without specialized knowledge.

- **Rapid Technological Change:** The constant evolution of technology means that security measures must continually adapt to new vulnerabilities and threats.

1.2 Why Everyday Users and Small Businesses Are at Risk

1.2.1 The Nature of Cyber Threats

Cyber threats come in many forms, ranging from sophisticated attacks on large corporations to seemingly small-scale scams targeting individuals. Common cyber threats include:

- **Phishing Attacks:** Deceptive emails or messages designed to trick users into revealing sensitive information, such as passwords or credit card numbers.

- **Malware and Ransomware:** Malicious software that can compromise your devices, encrypt your data, or even demand payment to restore access.

- **Social Engineering:** Tactics that exploit human psychology to gain access to personal data or secure systems.

- **Data Breaches:** Unauthorized access to databases where personal or financial information is stored, often resulting in identity theft or fraud.

1.2.2 The Vulnerability of Individuals and Small Businesses

While high-profile breaches often make headlines, everyday users and small businesses are prime targets for several reasons:

- **Limited Resources:** Unlike large enterprises, individuals and small businesses may not have dedicated IT security teams or robust security infrastructures.

- **Lack of Awareness:** Without a strong background in cybersecurity, many users underestimate the risks or fall prey to common tactics.

- **Interconnected Devices:** With the proliferation of IoT devices, even a small network can have multiple vulnerabilities, each providing a potential entry point for cybercriminals.

- **Economic Impact:** For small businesses, a single security breach can have devastating financial consequences, including loss of customer trust, legal liabilities, and operational disruptions.

1.2.3 Real-World Examples

Consider the following scenarios:

- **Personal Email Compromise:** An individual receives a seemingly innocuous email from a trusted source, which turns out to be a phishing attempt. Once the recipient clicks the link, malware is installed on their device, leading to a compromise of personal data.

- **Small Business Ransomware Attack:** A local business with limited cybersecurity measures falls victim to ransomware. Critical business files are encrypted, and the attackers demand a ransom for their release, potentially crippling the business's operations.

These examples illustrate that the risk is real and pervasive, affecting both personal and professional realms.

1.3 How This Guide Will Empower You to Protect Your Online Life

1.3.1 A Roadmap to Cybersecurity

This guide is designed to be a comprehensive resource for anyone looking to understand and implement cybersecurity best practices. Here's how it will help you:

- **Accessible Language:** Technical jargon is minimized, and complex concepts are broken down into easy-to-understand terms, ensuring that you can grasp the material regardless of your technical background.

- **Step-by-Step Instructions:** Each chapter provides actionable advice, clear steps, and practical examples that you can apply immediately to improve your digital security.

- **Holistic Approach:** The guide covers a broad range of topics—from safe browsing and device security to managing passwords and responding to cyber incidents—ensuring that all aspects of your online life are protected.

- **Adaptable Strategies:** Whether you're an individual user or a small business owner, the strategies presented here can be tailored to fit your specific needs and risk profile.

1.3.2 Building a Cybersecurity Mindset

Beyond technical measures, this guide emphasizes the importance of developing a proactive cybersecurity mindset. This involves:

- **Continuous Learning:** Cyber threats are always evolving. Staying informed and updated on the latest trends and techniques is crucial.

- **Risk Awareness:** Recognizing potential threats before they become issues is the first step in effective cybersecurity.

- **Preventative Action:** By adopting best practices and regular maintenance, you can significantly reduce your exposure to cyber risks.

1.3.3 What to Expect in the Coming Chapters

As you progress through this guide, you will:

- Gain a clear understanding of common cyber threats and how they operate.

- Learn how to secure your devices and protect your personal data with practical, step-by-step methods.

- Discover techniques for safe browsing, effective password management, and secure use of social media.

- Explore the unique challenges faced by small businesses and mobile users, with specialized strategies for each.

- Be equipped with the knowledge to respond to and recover from cyber incidents should they occur.

Conclusion

In this opening chapter, we've set the stage by exploring the dynamic and ever-expanding digital landscape, highlighting why both individuals and small businesses are increasingly at risk, and outlining how this guide will serve as your comprehensive resource for building robust cybersecurity practices. As you move forward, remember that cybersecurity is not a one-time fix but an ongoing commitment to vigilance, education, and proactive measures. The subsequent chapters will delve deeper into each area of cybersecurity, offering you the tools and knowledge to secure your digital life confidently.

Let's embark on this journey to create a safer, more secure digital environment—one step at a time.

Chapter 2: Understanding Cyber Threats

In this chapter, we will delve into the landscape of cyber threats that permeate our digital lives. By understanding what these threats are, how they operate, and the vulnerabilities they exploit, you'll be better prepared to recognize and defend against them. This comprehensive overview covers both the technical aspects and the human elements that often serve as the weak link in cybersecurity.

2.1 Overview of Cyber Threats

2.1.1 What Are Cyber Threats?

Cyber threats are malicious attempts to damage, steal, or disrupt digital information, networks, or devices. These threats can come in many forms, ranging from malicious software to sophisticated social engineering attacks. Their primary goal is often to exploit vulnerabilities—whether technical, procedural, or human—to gain unauthorized access or cause harm.

2.1.2 The Growing Importance of Understanding Cyber Threats

- **Increased Digital Dependency:** As individuals and businesses become more reliant on digital technologies, the potential impact of cyber threats grows.

- **Complex Attack Vectors:** Modern cyber attacks are multifaceted, combining technical exploits with human manipulation.

- **Evolving Threat Landscape:** Cybercriminals continuously update their methods, making it essential to stay informed about the latest tactics and vulnerabilities.

2.2 Common Cyber Threats

This section provides a detailed look at several of the most prevalent cyber threats that affect everyday users and small businesses.

2.2.1 Viruses and Malware

- **Definition and Types:**
  Malware (malicious software) is a broad term that includes various harmful programs such as viruses, worms, trojans, and more.

  - **Viruses:** Programs that attach themselves to legitimate software and spread to other programs or systems when executed.

  - **Worms:** Self-replicating malware that can spread independently over networks, often exploiting vulnerabilities in software.

- o **Trojans:** Malicious programs disguised as legitimate software, tricking users into installing them.

- **Impact:**
Malware can corrupt or delete data, steal sensitive information, and create backdoors for further exploitation.

2.2.2 Ransomware

- **How It Works:**
Ransomware is a type of malware that encrypts your files or locks you out of your device, then demands a ransom—usually in cryptocurrency—to restore access.

- **Key Characteristics:**

  - o **Encryption:** Your files become inaccessible until the ransom is paid.

  - o **Propagation:** Often spread through phishing emails or compromised websites.

  - o **High Impact:** Both individuals and businesses can suffer severe consequences, including data loss and operational downtime.

2.2.3 Phishing Attacks

- **Definition:**
  Phishing involves tricking users into revealing sensitive information (such as login credentials, credit card numbers, etc.) by masquerading as a trustworthy entity.

- **Variants:**

  - **Email Phishing:** The most common form, where fraudulent emails appear to be from reputable sources.

  - **Spear Phishing:** Highly targeted phishing attacks aimed at specific individuals or organizations.

  - **Smishing and Vishing:** Phishing attempts conducted via SMS (smishing) or voice calls (vishing).

- **Warning Signs:**

  - Unexpected requests for personal information

  - Poor grammar or spelling mistakes in messages

  - URLs that do not match the claimed source

2.2.4 Social Engineering

- **Concept:**
  Social engineering exploits human psychology rather than technical vulnerabilities. Attackers manipulate victims into making security mistakes or divulging confidential information.

- **Common Tactics:**

  - **Pretexting:** Creating a fabricated scenario to extract information.

  - **Baiting:** Offering something enticing (e.g., a free download) to lure victims into a trap.

  - **Tailgating:** Physically following someone into a secure location.

- **Impact:**
  Even the most secure technical systems can be compromised if an attacker successfully deceives a user.

2.2.5 Spyware and Adware

- **Spyware:**
  Software that secretly monitors your activities, often collecting sensitive data such as browsing habits, login credentials, or financial information.

- **Adware:**
  Software that displays unwanted advertisements,

which can sometimes come bundled with spyware. Though not always harmful on its own, it can degrade system performance and lead to privacy issues.

2.2.6 Denial-of-Service (DoS) and Distributed Denial-of-Service (DDoS) Attacks

- **DoS Attacks:**
  An attempt to make a network service unavailable by overwhelming it with traffic or sending information that triggers a crash.

- **DDoS Attacks:**
  Similar to DoS attacks, but originating from multiple sources (often a botnet), making them harder to block.

- **Impact on Businesses:**
  These attacks can disrupt operations, cause revenue loss, and damage an organization's reputation.

2.2.7 Advanced Persistent Threats (APTs)

- **Characteristics:**
  APTs involve long-term targeted attacks where the attacker gains unauthorized access to a network and remains undetected for an extended period.

- **Objectives:**
  These attacks are often carried out by organized groups (sometimes state-sponsored) seeking to

gather intelligence, disrupt operations, or exfiltrate sensitive data.

- **Complexity:**
APTs require significant resources and are usually aimed at large organizations, but understanding them is important because similar tactics can be applied on a smaller scale.

2.3 Real-World Examples of Cyber Attacks

2.3.1 The WannaCry Ransomware Attack

- **Overview:**
In 2017, the WannaCry ransomware attack affected hundreds of thousands of computers worldwide, including critical infrastructure such as hospitals.

- **Mechanism:**
It exploited a vulnerability in the Windows operating system, encrypting users' files and demanding ransom payments in Bitcoin.

- **Impact:**
The attack resulted in significant operational disruptions and highlighted the importance of keeping systems updated and patched.

2.3.2 Phishing Attacks on Financial Institutions

- **Scenario:**
  Many financial institutions have experienced phishing attacks where attackers impersonate bank officials, urging customers to verify their account information via fake websites.

- **Consequences:**
  Victims often end up disclosing sensitive data, leading to unauthorized transactions and identity theft.

- **Lessons Learned:**
  The prevalence of such attacks reinforces the need for robust authentication methods and user education on recognizing suspicious communications.

2.3.3 Social Engineering in Corporate Environments

- **Case Study:**
  A well-known corporation once fell victim to a social engineering attack where an attacker, posing as a trusted vendor, convinced an employee to grant access to sensitive systems.

- **Outcome:**
  The breach resulted in the theft of proprietary information and a costly investigation.

- **Prevention:**
  This case emphasizes the importance of verifying identities and implementing strict access controls.

2.4 How Attackers Exploit Vulnerabilities

2.4.1 Technical Vulnerabilities

- **Outdated Software and Systems:**
  Unpatched operating systems and applications are prime targets for exploitation. Cybercriminals frequently scan for systems with known vulnerabilities.

- **Misconfigurations:**
  Incorrectly configured networks or devices (e.g., unsecured Wi-Fi, default passwords) can provide an easy entry point.

- **Zero-Day Exploits:**
  These are vulnerabilities that are unknown to the software vendor and have not yet been patched, making them particularly dangerous when discovered by attackers.

2.4.2 Human Factors

- **Weak Passwords:**
  Simple or reused passwords make it easier for attackers to gain unauthorized access through brute force or credential stuffing.

- **Lack of Awareness:**
  Users who are not informed about the latest cyber threats may inadvertently click on malicious links or fall for scams.

- **Social Engineering:**
  Exploiting human trust and curiosity, attackers manipulate victims into providing access or divulging confidential information.

2.4.3 Organizational Vulnerabilities

- **Insufficient Security Policies:**
  Organizations without clear cybersecurity protocols or employee training programs are more vulnerable to attacks.

- **Inadequate Monitoring:**
  Without regular security audits and monitoring, suspicious activities may go unnoticed until significant damage has been done.

- **Resource Constraints:**
  Small businesses, in particular, may lack the resources for robust cybersecurity measures, making them attractive targets for cybercriminals.

2.5 Summary

In this chapter, we have explored the multifaceted world of cyber threats, from the common types like malware, ransomware, and phishing, to more sophisticated attacks such as APTs. We examined real-world examples that illustrate the severe consequences of these attacks and delved into the various vulnerabilities—technical, human, and organizational—that attackers exploit. Understanding these threats is the first step in developing effective strategies to combat them, setting the stage for the more hands-on protection measures discussed in later chapters.

By familiarizing yourself with these concepts, you build a solid foundation to recognize potential risks and take proactive steps to defend your digital environment. In the following chapters, we will translate this understanding into actionable practices, ensuring you are well-equipped to safeguard your personal and professional data.

With this comprehensive view of cyber threats, you are now better prepared to delve deeper into the tactics and tools that will help you secure your digital life. Let's move forward with the knowledge that vigilance and informed action are key to preventing and mitigating cyber attacks.

Chapter 3: Demystifying Cybersecurity Concepts

Understanding cybersecurity can feel overwhelming, especially when bombarded with technical jargon. In this chapter, we break down the key concepts and terminology used in cybersecurity into accessible, everyday language. By the end of this chapter, you'll have a clear grasp of the foundational elements that form the backbone of modern cybersecurity practices, empowering you to make informed decisions about protecting your digital life.

3.1 Introduction to Cybersecurity Concepts

Cybersecurity encompasses a broad range of technologies, processes, and practices designed to safeguard computers, networks, and data from unauthorized access and malicious attacks. Rather than getting lost in technical details, this chapter aims to:

- **Explain Core Concepts:** Introduce you to the fundamental terminology and mechanisms that underlie cybersecurity.

- **Simplify Technical Jargon:** Translate complex ideas into everyday language, using relatable analogies.

- **Build Confidence:** Help you understand that you don't need to be an expert to implement effective security measures.

3.2 Key Terminology and Concepts

In this section, we detail the essential cybersecurity terms that you will encounter throughout this guide. Understanding these concepts will serve as the building blocks for implementing security measures in your daily digital interactions.

3.2.1 Encryption

Definition:
Encryption is the process of converting information or data into a code to prevent unauthorized access. Think of it as locking your data in a safe that can only be opened with the correct key.

Key Points:

- **Symmetric Encryption:** Uses the same key for both encrypting and decrypting data. It's fast and efficient but requires secure key sharing.

- **Asymmetric Encryption:** Uses a pair of keys—a public key for encryption and a private key for decryption. This method is more secure for sharing information over insecure channels.

- **Everyday Use:** When you see a padlock icon in your browser's address bar (HTTPS), it indicates that the data exchanged with that site is encrypted.

3.2.2 Firewalls

Definition:

A firewall is a security system that monitors and controls incoming and outgoing network traffic based on predetermined security rules. It acts as a barrier between your trusted internal network and untrusted external networks, such as the internet.

Key Points:

- **Types of Firewalls:** Software firewalls (installed on individual devices) and hardware firewalls (physical devices that protect networks).

- **Functionality:** Firewalls block malicious traffic, filter data packets, and prevent unauthorized access.

- **Everyday Use:** Many home routers include built-in firewall features to protect your personal network from external threats.

3.2.3 Virtual Private Networks (VPNs)

Definition:

A Virtual Private Network (VPN) creates a secure, encrypted connection over a less secure network, such as the internet. It's like having a private, secure tunnel for your data.

Key Points:

- **Security Benefits:** VPNs protect your data from interception, especially when using public Wi-Fi networks.

- **Privacy Benefits:** They mask your IP address and location, enhancing your online privacy.

- **Everyday Use:** VPNs are useful for remote workers, travelers, or anyone wanting to add an extra layer of security when browsing the internet.

3.2.4 Anti-Virus and Anti-Malware Software

Definition:
These are programs designed to detect, prevent, and remove malicious software (malware) from your devices.

Key Points:

- **Detection Methods:** Regular scans, real-time monitoring, and signature-based detection help identify threats.

- **Proactive Protection:** Many programs also use heuristics and behavioral analysis to detect new, unknown threats.

- **Everyday Use:** Installing reputable anti-virus software and keeping it updated is one of the simplest ways to protect your devices from malware.

3.2.5 Intrusion Detection Systems (IDS) and Intrusion Prevention Systems (IPS)

Definition:

IDS and IPS are systems that monitor network traffic for suspicious activity. An IDS alerts you to potential threats, while an IPS takes proactive measures to block or prevent the detected threats.

Key Points:

- **IDS:** Acts as an alarm system that notifies administrators of possible breaches.

- **IPS:** Goes a step further by automatically blocking detected threats.

- **Everyday Use:** While more common in business environments, understanding these systems can help you appreciate the layers of defense available for your network.

3.2.6 Security Patches and Updates

Definition:

Security patches are updates released by software vendors to fix vulnerabilities and improve security.

Key Points:

- **Importance:** Regularly updating software ensures that known vulnerabilities are patched, reducing the risk of exploitation.

- **Automatic Updates:** Many systems and applications offer automatic update features to simplify this process.

- **Everyday Use:** Always install updates for your operating system, browsers, and applications to keep your devices secure.

3.2.7 Two-Factor Authentication (2FA) and Multi-Factor Authentication (MFA)

Definition:
2FA and MFA add extra layers of security to your login process by requiring additional verification beyond just a password.

Key Points:

- **How It Works:** After entering your password, you must provide a second form of verification (e.g., a code sent to your phone).

- **Benefits:** This significantly reduces the risk of unauthorized access even if your password is compromised.

- **Everyday Use:** Enable 2FA or MFA on all accounts that offer it, particularly email, banking, and social media accounts.

3.2.8 Public Key Infrastructure (PKI)

Definition:

PKI is a framework for managing digital certificates and public-key encryption. It ensures that the identities of the parties exchanging information are verified.

Key Points:

- **Digital Certificates:** These are like electronic passports that verify the ownership of a public key.

- **Trust Models:** PKI helps establish trust between parties by relying on trusted certificate authorities (CAs).

- **Everyday Use:** PKI underlies many secure online transactions and communications, ensuring that you're interacting with legitimate websites and services.

3.2.9 Additional Concepts

Other important cybersecurity concepts include:

- **Biometrics:** Using unique biological characteristics (e.g., fingerprints, facial recognition) for identification and access control.

- **Sandboxing:** Running applications in isolated environments to prevent potential threats from affecting the entire system.

- **Data Backups:** Regularly saving copies of your data in secure locations to recover information in case of loss or attack.

3.3 How Cybersecurity Works in Layman's Terms

Translating these concepts into everyday language can make them more relatable:

- **Encryption as a Secret Code:** Imagine sending a message in a secret code that only you and the recipient know. Even if someone intercepts it, they can't understand it without the key.

- **Firewalls as Security Guards:** Think of a firewall as a security guard stationed at the entrance of a building, checking IDs and ensuring that only authorized individuals can enter.

- **VPNs as Private Tunnels:** Using a VPN is like traveling through a private tunnel that shields you from prying eyes on a busy highway.

- **Anti-Virus Software as a Health Check-Up:** Regular scans by anti-virus software are akin to routine health check-ups, ensuring that your devices are free from harmful infections.

- **2FA as Double-Locking Your Door:** Enabling 2FA is similar to having a deadbolt in addition to your regular door lock, making unauthorized entry much more difficult.

By drawing these parallels, the technical mechanisms of cybersecurity become more tangible and easier to grasp.

3.4 Dispelling Myths and Common Misconceptions

There are several pervasive myths about cybersecurity that can lead to complacency. Here, we address and debunk some of the most common misconceptions:

Myth 1: "Cybersecurity Is Only for IT Experts"

- **Reality:**
  Cybersecurity measures can be implemented by anyone. Basic practices such as updating software, using strong passwords, and enabling 2FA can dramatically improve your security, even without advanced technical knowledge.

Myth 2: "I'm Too Small or Unimportant to Be Targeted"

- **Reality:**
  Cybercriminals often target individuals and small businesses precisely because they are less likely to have robust security measures in place. No one is immune from cyber threats.

Myth 3: "I Have Nothing to Hide, So I Don't Need to Worry"

- **Reality:**
  Cybersecurity isn't just about hiding secrets—it's about protecting your identity, financial assets, and personal information. Even if you believe you have nothing to hide, your data can be misused in ways you might not anticipate.

Myth 4: "Antivirus Software Alone Is Enough to Keep Me Safe"

- **Reality:**
  While antivirus software is a critical component of cybersecurity, it should be part of a layered approach. Combining antivirus software with firewalls, VPNs, regular updates, and strong authentication practices provides much more comprehensive protection.

3.5 Practical Applications of Cybersecurity Concepts

Understanding these concepts is only the first step; applying them in everyday situations is what truly makes a difference. Here are some practical tips:

- **Implement Encryption:** Use encrypted messaging apps for private conversations and ensure that sensitive data is stored in encrypted formats.

- **Configure Firewalls:** Ensure that your home router's firewall is enabled and properly configured to block unauthorized access.

- **Utilize VPNs:** Install a reputable VPN, especially when connecting to public Wi-Fi networks, to secure your internet traffic.

- **Keep Software Updated:** Regularly check for and install software updates and patches to close security vulnerabilities.

- **Enable 2FA/MFA:** Add an extra layer of protection to your online accounts by enabling two-factor or multi-factor authentication wherever possible.

- **Adopt a Backup Strategy:** Regularly back up important files—either to the cloud or an external drive—to ensure you can recover your data if it's ever compromised.

3.6 Conclusion

This chapter has stripped away much of the complexity of cybersecurity by breaking down its key concepts and terms into everyday language. By understanding the roles of encryption, firewalls, VPNs, anti-virus software, and other essential components, you now have a solid foundation to appreciate how various security measures work together to protect your digital life.

Furthermore, by debunking common myths, you're better positioned to adopt a proactive approach to security—realizing that effective cybersecurity is not reserved for experts but is within everyone's reach. In the next chapters, we will build upon this foundation by discussing how to apply these concepts practically, ensuring that your everyday online activities are secure and resilient against evolving cyber threats.

Armed with this newfound knowledge, you are now ready to transition from theory to practice. The journey to securing your digital world continues with practical strategies and step-by-step guidance in the chapters that follow.

Chapter 4: Safe Browsing and Internet Hygiene

In an era where the internet is woven into nearly every aspect of daily life, safe browsing and maintaining good internet hygiene have become essential practices for protecting your digital footprint. This chapter provides a detailed guide on how to navigate the web securely, covering everything from configuring your browser's security settings to identifying malicious websites and practicing proactive online habits.

4.1 The Importance of Safe Browsing

4.1.1 Defining Safe Browsing

Safe browsing refers to the practice of navigating the internet in a manner that minimizes exposure to security threats. This includes being cautious of the websites you visit, the links you click, and the data you share online. A secure browsing experience not only protects your device from malware and viruses but also helps safeguard your personal information from being compromised.

4.1.2 Why Internet Hygiene Matters

Internet hygiene is a set of behaviors and practices designed to maintain the cleanliness and security of your digital life. Much like personal hygiene helps keep you healthy, good internet hygiene prevents digital infections and cyber threats. This includes:

- Regularly updating software and browsers.

- Clearing cookies and cache to prevent tracking.

- Managing passwords and sensitive information.

- Being aware of phishing and scam attempts.

Adopting safe browsing habits can significantly reduce the likelihood of encountering harmful content and falling victim to cyberattacks.

4.2 Configuring Browser Security Settings

4.2.1 Choosing a Secure Browser

While many modern browsers come with built-in security features, it's important to choose one that prioritizes privacy and regular security updates. Popular browsers such as Google Chrome, Mozilla Firefox, and Microsoft Edge offer robust security tools. Consider these factors when selecting a browser:

- Frequency of updates.

- Availability of security extensions.

- Customizable privacy settings.

- Transparency regarding data collection practices.

4.2.2 Adjusting Privacy and Security Settings

Once you've chosen a browser, adjust its settings to enhance security:

- **Enable Pop-Up Blockers:** Prevent unwanted pop-ups that might contain malware or phishing links.

- **Disable Third-Party Cookies:** Limit tracking by blocking cookies from websites that you do not directly visit.

- **Use Secure DNS:** Enable DNS over HTTPS (DoH) if your browser supports it to encrypt DNS requests.

- **Set Up Content Filters:** Some browsers allow you to block malicious websites and filter out potentially dangerous content.

4.2.3 Managing Browser Extensions and Add-Ons

Extensions can significantly enhance your browsing experience, but they also introduce potential security risks:

- **Install Trusted Extensions:** Only download extensions from reputable sources or official browser stores.

- **Review Permissions:** Be cautious of extensions that request access to all your data or sensitive information.

- **Regularly Audit Installed Extensions:** Periodically review and remove extensions that are no longer needed or are outdated.

4.3 Recognizing and Avoiding Malicious Websites and Links

4.3.1 Identifying Suspicious URLs and Website Indicators

Malicious websites often mimic legitimate sites to trick users into divulging sensitive information. To recognize potential threats:

- **Check the URL:** Look for misspellings or unusual characters. Secure sites should begin with "https://" and display a padlock icon in the address bar.

- **Examine the Website Design:** Poor design quality, broken links, or an overwhelming number of ads can be indicators of a fraudulent website.

- **Use Online Tools:** Utilize services like Google Safe Browsing or VirusTotal to check if a website has been flagged for suspicious activity.

4.3.2 Avoiding Phishing and Scam Links

Phishing attacks are designed to lure you into providing sensitive information:

- **Hover Over Links:** Before clicking, hover your cursor over a link to preview its destination. If the URL looks suspicious or unfamiliar, do not click it.

- **Be Wary of Urgent Messages:** Emails or messages that urge immediate action, particularly those asking for personal data, are often phishing attempts.

- **Verify the Source:** If you receive an unexpected request from a known entity, contact them directly using a verified method rather than replying to the message.

4.3.3 Safe Download Practices

Downloading files from the internet can introduce malware if not done carefully:

- **Download from Official Sources:** Always obtain software and files from official websites or trusted app stores.

- **Scan Downloads:** Use reputable antivirus software to scan files before opening them.

- **Avoid Unsolicited Downloads:** Be cautious of unsolicited file downloads, especially if prompted by unfamiliar websites or email attachments.

4.4 Tools and Browser Extensions to Enhance Security

4.4.1 Recommended Security Tools

Several tools and extensions can improve your browsing safety:

- **Ad Blockers:** Tools like uBlock Origin or Adblock Plus can prevent intrusive ads and reduce the risk of malvertising.

- **Anti-Tracking Extensions:** Privacy-focused extensions, such as Privacy Badger or Ghostery, block trackers that collect your browsing data.

- **Secure Password Managers:** Integrate password managers like LastPass, 1Password, or Bitwarden with your browser to store and autofill strong, unique passwords securely.

- **Script Blockers:** Extensions like NoScript (for advanced users) allow you to control which scripts run on websites, reducing the risk of drive-by downloads and other malicious activities.

4.4.2 Enhancing Security with VPNs

A Virtual Private Network (VPN) not only protects your data when connected to public Wi-Fi but can also enhance your privacy by masking your IP address and encrypting your internet traffic. Consider reputable VPN services that offer robust encryption, a no-logs policy, and regular security audits.

4.5 Browsing on Public Wi-Fi and Mobile Devices

4.5.1 Risks of Public Wi-Fi

Public Wi-Fi networks, found in cafes, airports, and hotels, are often unsecured and can be breeding grounds for cybercriminals:

- **Data Interception:** Without encryption, attackers can intercept data transmitted over public networks.

- **Rogue Hotspots:** Cybercriminals may set up fake Wi-Fi networks with similar names to legitimate ones to capture sensitive information.

4.5.2 Safe Practices on Public Networks

- **Use a VPN:** Always connect to a VPN when using public Wi-Fi to secure your connection.

- **Avoid Sensitive Transactions:** Refrain from accessing bank accounts or entering sensitive information on public networks.

- **Turn Off Sharing:** Disable file sharing and other network discovery features when connected to public Wi-Fi.

4.5.3 Mobile Browsing Considerations

Mobile devices are equally vulnerable:

- **Update Regularly:** Keep your mobile operating system and apps updated with the latest security patches.

- **Install Security Apps:** Consider installing mobile security apps that offer features like malware scanning and safe browsing.

- **Monitor App Permissions:** Regularly review and manage app permissions to ensure apps do not have access to unnecessary data.

4.6 Developing Good Internet Hygiene Habits

4.6.1 Regular Maintenance and Updates

Keeping your digital environment clean is an ongoing process:

- **Clear Cache and Cookies:** Regularly clear your browser's cache and cookies to remove potentially harmful data and tracking information.

- **Update Software:** Ensure your browser, operating system, and security software are always up to date.

- **Backup Data:** Maintain regular backups of important data, either to a secure cloud service or an external drive.

4.6.2 Mindful Navigation and Online Behavior

Developing a mindful approach to your online activities can reduce risk:

- **Think Before You Click:** Be cautious about clicking on unknown links or pop-up ads.

- **Use Bookmarking:** Instead of relying on search engine results that might lead to dubious sites, bookmark trusted websites.

- **Verify Before Sharing:** Double-check the authenticity of information before sharing or forwarding it, especially on social media.

4.6.3 Educating Yourself and Others

Stay informed about new online threats and share your knowledge:

- **Follow Cybersecurity News:** Regularly read updates from reputable sources to stay aware of emerging threats.

- **Participate in Online Communities:** Engage in forums and groups dedicated to cybersecurity to exchange tips and experiences.

- **Train Family and Colleagues:** Share best practices with those around you, fostering a culture of cybersecurity awareness.

4.7 Conclusion

Safe browsing and maintaining good internet hygiene are critical components of your overall cybersecurity strategy. By configuring your browser settings, recognizing and avoiding malicious websites, and using supportive security tools, you can dramatically reduce your risk of falling victim to cyber threats. Additionally, adopting mindful online habits—whether on public Wi-Fi or mobile devices—ensures that you remain vigilant in an ever-evolving digital landscape.

In this chapter, you've learned:

- How to set up and manage browser security settings.

- The techniques for identifying malicious links and websites.

- The importance of tools like VPNs, ad blockers, and anti-tracking extensions.

- Best practices for navigating public networks and mobile environments.

- How regular maintenance and informed online behavior contribute to a secure digital life.

Armed with these strategies, you are now better equipped to enjoy the vast opportunities of the internet while keeping your personal data safe and secure. As we move forward, the next chapters will continue to build on these concepts by exploring device-specific security practices and advanced strategies to protect your online presence.

Let's continue on the journey toward a safer and more secure digital experience.

Chapter 5: Securing Your Devices

Our devices—be they desktop computers, laptops, smartphones, tablets, or smart home gadgets—serve as the gateways to your digital life. Securing these devices is paramount because even the most robust online practices can be undermined if your device is compromised. In this chapter, we will explore detailed, actionable steps to protect every type of device you use. From routine maintenance and software updates to advanced configuration settings, this guide provides a comprehensive look at safeguarding your digital tools.

5.1 Why Device Security Matters

5.1.1 The Role of Devices in Cybersecurity

Your devices are not just passive tools; they actively store, process, and transmit your personal and sensitive data. When these devices are insecure, they become vulnerable entry points for cybercriminals. Whether through malware infections, unauthorized access, or data breaches, a compromised device can expose you to risks that extend far beyond just a single piece of information.

5.1.2 The Consequences of Insecure Devices

- **Data Loss or Theft:** Sensitive personal and financial information can be stolen.

- **Malware Infections:** Viruses and other malicious software can damage system files, slow down performance, or hijack your device for further attacks.

- **Unauthorized Access:** Cybercriminals may use insecure devices as launchpads to access your other accounts or networks.

- **Network Vulnerabilities:** An insecure device on your home or business network can serve as a backdoor for wider network breaches.

5.2 Securing Desktop and Laptop Computers

Desktop and laptop computers often serve as the central hubs for work, personal projects, and online communications. Securing these devices involves a combination of software management, system configuration, and user habits.

5.2.1 Operating System and Software Updates

- **Regular Updates:** Ensure that your operating system (Windows, macOS, Linux, etc.) is set to update automatically. Updates often include security patches that close vulnerabilities.

- **Application Updates:** In addition to the OS, regularly update all installed applications, including browsers, productivity tools, and media players.

- **End-of-Life Software:** Avoid using outdated software that no longer receives security updates.

5.2.2 Antivirus and Anti-Malware Protection

- **Install Trusted Software:** Use reputable antivirus and anti-malware programs that offer real-time protection and regular scanning.

- **Scheduled Scans:** Set up automatic scans to check for malware regularly.

- **Heuristic Analysis:** Ensure your antivirus solution uses heuristic techniques to detect previously unknown threats.

5.2.3 Firewalls and Network Security

- **Enable Firewalls:** Use the built-in firewall on your operating system or install a third-party firewall to monitor incoming and outgoing traffic.

- **Configure Router Settings:** Secure your network by updating your router's firmware, changing default passwords, and disabling remote management features.

- **Network Segmentation:** For enhanced security, consider segmenting your network—keeping critical systems and less secure devices on separate subnetworks.

5.2.4 User Account Management

- **Administrator vs. Standard Accounts:** Use standard user accounts for everyday tasks and reserve administrator accounts for system changes.

- **Password Policies:** Implement strong, unique passwords for all accounts and consider using a password manager.

- **Biometric Options:** Where available, enable biometric authentication (fingerprint or facial recognition) for an added layer of security.

5.2.5 Data Encryption and Backup

- **Full-Disk Encryption:** Use full-disk encryption tools (like BitLocker for Windows or FileVault for macOS) to protect data on your hard drive.

- **Regular Backups:** Schedule regular backups of critical data to an external drive or a trusted cloud service. Ensure backups are also secure and encrypted.

- **Backup Testing:** Periodically test your backups to verify that data can be successfully restored in the event of a breach or hardware failure.

5.3 Securing Mobile Devices

Smartphones and tablets have become indispensable, but their portability also makes them prime targets for cyber threats. Securing mobile devices requires attention to software, settings, and behavioral practices.

5.3.1 Keeping the Operating System Updated

- **Automatic Updates:** Enable automatic updates to ensure your mobile operating system (iOS, Android, etc.) receives the latest security patches.

- **App Store Integrity:** Download apps only from official app stores to minimize the risk of installing malicious software.

5.3.2 Application Security and Permissions

- **Review App Permissions:** Regularly check the permissions granted to each app and revoke any that seem excessive for the app's functionality.

- **App Reviews and Ratings:** Before downloading a new app, review its ratings, feedback, and the reputation of the developer.

- **Security-Focused Apps:** Consider installing reputable security apps that offer malware scanning, remote wipe capabilities, and phone location tracking.

5.3.3 Secure Communication

- **Encrypted Messaging:** Use messaging apps that offer end-to-end encryption to secure your conversations.

- **VPN for Mobile:** Consider installing a VPN on your mobile device to protect data transmitted over public or unsecured networks.

- **Two-Factor Authentication:** Enable two-factor authentication on apps and services that support it, adding a layer of protection to your accounts.

5.3.4 Device Access and Recovery

- **Lock Screen Security:** Use strong PINs, passwords, or biometric locks to secure your device's lock screen.

- **Remote Wipe and Tracking:** Activate features that allow you to remotely locate or wipe your device if it is lost or stolen.

- **SIM Card Security:** Set up a SIM card lock to prevent unauthorized use if your device is misplaced.

5.4 Securing IoT and Smart Home Devices

The proliferation of Internet of Things (IoT) devices—from smart thermostats to security cameras—introduces unique security challenges. These devices often have limited processing power and may not receive regular updates.

5.4.1 Changing Default Credentials

- **Default Passwords:** Immediately change any default usernames and passwords on IoT devices, as these are widely known and exploited by attackers.

- **Unique Credentials:** Use strong, unique passwords for each device to prevent a single compromised device from endangering your entire network.

5.4.2 Firmware Updates

- **Regular Checks:** Regularly check for firmware updates for all IoT devices. Manufacturers frequently release patches to address security vulnerabilities.

- **Automatic Updates:** Where available, enable automatic firmware updates to ensure your devices are always running the latest security software.

5.4.3 Network Segmentation for IoT

- **Separate Networks:** Consider placing IoT devices on a separate network from your primary computers and mobile devices. This limits the potential damage if an IoT device is compromised.

- **Guest Networks:** Many modern routers allow you to set up guest networks specifically for IoT devices, keeping them isolated from critical systems.

5.4.4 Monitoring and Managing IoT Devices

- **Regular Audits:** Periodically review the list of connected IoT devices on your network. Remove any devices that are no longer in use.

- **Secure Configurations:** Ensure that device settings are configured for maximum security, even if it means sacrificing some convenience.

- **Vendor Reputation:** Purchase IoT devices from reputable vendors known for providing regular security updates and robust support.

5.5 Best Practices and Additional Tips for Device Security

5.5.1 Practice the Principle of Least Privilege

- **Limit Access:** Only grant the minimum permissions required for apps and services to function properly.

- **Regular Reviews:** Periodically audit permissions and access rights to ensure they remain appropriate over time.

5.5.2 Educate Yourself and Others

- **Stay Informed:** Keep up with the latest security trends and threats affecting your devices.

- **Training:** Educate family members or employees on safe device practices, including the importance of updates, strong passwords, and recognizing phishing attempts.

5.5.3 Physical Security

- **Device Location:** Be mindful of where your devices are physically located. Do not leave laptops or smartphones unattended in public places.

- **Secure Storage:** When not in use, store devices in a secure location, and consider physical locks for desktop computers in office settings.

5.5.4 Multi-Layered Security Approach

- **Combine Measures:** Rely on a combination of software tools (antivirus, firewalls, encryption) and safe usage habits.

- **Regular Assessments:** Periodically evaluate your security measures to ensure they are effective and up-to-date.

5.6 Conclusion

Securing your devices is a critical component of your overall cybersecurity strategy. Whether you're using a desktop, laptop, smartphone, or a myriad of IoT gadgets, the steps outlined in this chapter provide a robust framework to protect your digital life. By staying vigilant, keeping your software updated, using strong authentication methods, and following best practices for network and device management, you can significantly reduce your exposure to cyber threats.

As you move forward, remember that device security is not a one-time effort but an ongoing process that adapts to new challenges and technologies. The next chapters will build on these foundations, exploring more advanced strategies and specialized scenarios to help you maintain a secure digital environment in every aspect of your online life.

Chapter 6: Mastering Passwords and Authentication

Passwords and authentication are the first line of defense in securing your digital life. In a world where a single compromised password can open the door to personal data, financial information, and even entire networks, understanding and implementing robust password and authentication strategies is essential. This chapter provides a comprehensive guide to creating, managing, and strengthening your passwords and authentication methods, ensuring that your digital identity remains secure.

6.1 The Critical Role of Passwords in Cybersecurity

6.1.1 Passwords as the Frontline Defense

Passwords serve as the primary barrier between your private information and cybercriminals. They protect access to email, banking, social media, and countless other services. A strong password not only keeps unauthorized users out but also acts as a foundational element of your overall security posture.

6.1.2 The Consequences of Weak Passwords

- **Data Breaches:** Compromised passwords can lead to unauthorized access, resulting in data breaches that affect your personal and professional life.

- **Identity Theft:** Weak or reused passwords can allow cybercriminals to assume your identity, leading to financial loss and reputational damage.

- **Cascade Failures:** When passwords are reused across multiple accounts, a breach in one area can lead to a domino effect, compromising your entire digital ecosystem.

6.2 Creating Strong, Resilient Passwords

6.2.1 Characteristics of a Strong Password

A robust password typically exhibits the following traits:

- **Length:** Aim for a minimum of 12 to 16 characters.

- **Complexity:** Combine uppercase and lowercase letters, numbers, and special symbols.

- **Uniqueness:** Use different passwords for different accounts to prevent one breach from compromising multiple services.

- **Unpredictability:** Avoid common words, phrases, or easily guessable sequences such as "password123" or "qwerty."

6.2.2 Best Practices for Crafting Passwords

- **Avoid Personal Information:** Do not include easily accessible details like birthdays, names, or pet names.

- **Use a Passphrase:** Create a long string of words or a sentence that is easy for you to remember but hard for others to guess. For example, "BlueSky$Morning!RunFast#2025" combines a phrase with special characters.

- **Randomness is Key:** Consider using a password generator to create complex, unpredictable passwords.

6.2.3 The Do's and Don'ts of Password Creation

- **Do:**
    - Use a mix of character types.
    - Create a unique password for every account.
    - Change passwords periodically, especially after any suspected breach.

- **Don't:**
    - Reuse the same password across multiple sites.
    - Write passwords down in an easily accessible location.
    - Use sequential letters or numbers.

6.3 Password Managers: Simplifying Security

6.3.1 What Are Password Managers?

Password managers are software tools designed to securely store and manage your passwords. They generate complex passwords, auto-fill login credentials, and encrypt your password database with a master password.

6.3.2 Benefits of Using a Password Manager

- **Enhanced Security:** They allow you to create and store unique, complex passwords for every account without the need to remember each one.

- **Convenience:** Auto-fill features streamline the login process while keeping your credentials secure.

- **Centralized Management:** Easily update, audit, and change your passwords from one secure location.

- **Cross-Platform Support:** Many password managers offer apps and browser extensions that sync across devices, ensuring your passwords are accessible wherever you go.

6.3.3 Choosing a Password Manager

Consider the following when selecting a password manager:

- **Security Features:** Look for strong encryption standards (e.g., AES-256) and multi-factor authentication options.

- **User Interface:** Ensure it is user-friendly and integrates seamlessly with your devices and browsers.

- **Reputation and Reviews:** Research the vendor's history, update frequency, and overall community trust.

- **Cost vs. Features:** Some managers offer robust free versions, while others require a subscription for advanced features.

6.4 Multi-Factor and Two-Factor Authentication

6.4.1 Understanding Multi-Factor Authentication (MFA)

Multi-factor authentication (MFA) is a security measure that requires more than one method of verification to access an account. By combining multiple factors, MFA significantly reduces the likelihood of unauthorized access.

6.4.2 Types of Authentication Factors

- **Something You Know:** Passwords or PINs.

- **Something You Have:** A physical device, such as a smartphone (for SMS codes or authenticator apps) or a hardware token.

- **Something You Are:** Biometric factors like fingerprints, facial recognition, or voice recognition.

6.4.3 Implementing Two-Factor Authentication (2FA)

Two-factor authentication (2FA) is a subset of MFA that requires exactly two forms of verification:

- **SMS or Email Codes:** A temporary code sent to your phone or email.

- **Authenticator Apps:** Applications like Google Authenticator or Authy that generate time-sensitive codes.

- **Hardware Tokens:** Physical devices (e.g., YubiKey) that provide secure, one-time codes.

- **Biometrics:** Using a fingerprint or facial recognition as an additional verification step.

6.4.4 Advantages of MFA/2FA

- **Increased Security:** Even if a password is compromised, the additional factor provides an extra layer of protection.

- **Reduced Risk of Phishing:** Attackers are less likely to succeed if they need access to your physical device or biometric data.

- **Ease of Implementation:** Many online services now offer built-in MFA options, making it simple to add this extra layer of security.

6.5 Maintaining and Updating Your Authentication Practices

6.5.1 Regular Password Updates

- **Scheduled Changes:** Regularly update your passwords, especially for critical accounts like banking or email.

- **Post-Breach Protocols:** Immediately change passwords if a service you use experiences a data breach.

- **Avoid Frequent Reuse:** While it is important to update passwords, avoid recycling old passwords to ensure maximum security.

6.5.2 Monitoring and Auditing Your Accounts

- **Security Check-Ups:** Periodically review the security settings of your accounts, checking for any unauthorized changes.

- **Account Activity:** Regularly inspect account activity logs where available, to detect any anomalies or suspicious login attempts.

6.5.3 Educating Yourself and Staying Informed

- **Stay Updated:** Cybersecurity is an ever-evolving field. Follow trusted sources and cybersecurity news to remain informed about the latest threats and best practices.

- **Continuous Improvement:** Be open to adopting new authentication methods as technology advances, such as behavioral biometrics or passwordless authentication.

6.6 Best Practices for Account Recovery

6.6.1 Secure Recovery Options

- **Backup Email/Phone:** Ensure your account recovery options (such as backup email addresses or phone numbers) are up to date and secured.

- **Security Questions:** Use challenging security questions that aren't easily guessable. When possible, choose custom questions with answers only you would know.

- **Two-Step Recovery:** Opt for recovery methods that require more than one verification step to prevent unauthorized resets.

6.6.2 Preparing for the Unexpected

- **Document Critical Information:** Securely record details related to account recovery in a password manager.

- **Plan for Compromise:** Know the steps to take if you lose access to an account, including contacting support and verifying your identity through multiple channels.

6.7 The Future of Authentication

6.7.1 Emerging Technologies

- **Biometric Advancements:** Future developments in biometric technology may include more accurate and less invasive methods such as vein pattern recognition or behavioral biometrics.

- **Passwordless Authentication:** Innovations like cryptographic keys and single sign-on (SSO) solutions are reducing the reliance on traditional passwords.

- **Decentralized Identity:** Blockchain-based solutions are emerging as potential tools for secure, decentralized authentication, giving users more control over their digital identities.

6.7.2 The Evolving Threat Landscape

- **Adaptive Authentication:** Systems are increasingly using artificial intelligence to detect unusual login behavior and adapt authentication requirements in real time.

- **Integration and Interoperability:** As more devices and services connect, integrated security solutions that combine multiple authentication methods will become standard.

6.8 Conclusion

Mastering passwords and authentication is a critical step in building a robust cybersecurity foundation. By creating strong, unique passwords, leveraging password managers, and implementing multi-factor authentication, you significantly reduce the risk of unauthorized access to your accounts. In this chapter, you have learned:

- The importance of passwords as the first barrier against cyber threats.

- How to create and manage strong, complex passwords.

- The benefits and features of using password managers.

- How multi-factor authentication adds critical layers

.

of security.

- Best practices for maintaining, updating, and recovering your authentication credentials.

- Insights into emerging authentication technologies that will shape the future of cybersecurity.

As you continue to secure your digital life, remember that the strength of your security is only as robust as your weakest password or authentication method. Keep these practices at the forefront of your cybersecurity strategy, and continually adapt as technology and threats evolve. In the next chapter, we will explore methods for protecting your personal data and privacy in an increasingly interconnected world.

Chapter 7: Protecting Your Personal Data and Privacy

In today's digital era, personal data is one of your most valuable assets—and one of the most attractive targets for cybercriminals. This chapter provides an in-depth look at what personal data encompasses, the various threats to your privacy, and actionable strategies to safeguard your information. Whether you're managing sensitive financial records, social media profiles, or everyday communications, the principles and practices outlined here will help you build a robust defense against unauthorized access and misuse of your data.

7.1 Introduction to Personal Data and Privacy

7.1.1 Defining Personal Data and Privacy

- **Personal Data:** This refers to any information that can be used to identify an individual. It includes basic details such as your name, address, and email, as well as more sensitive information like social security numbers, financial records, and medical history.

- **Privacy:** At its core, privacy is about controlling who has access to your personal information and how it is used. It involves ensuring that your data is not disclosed, misused, or exploited without your consent.

7.1.2 Why Protecting Personal Data Matters

- **Risk of Identity Theft:** Cybercriminals can use personal data to impersonate you, open fraudulent accounts, or commit financial fraud.

- **Privacy Invasion:** Unwanted access to personal data can lead to a loss of privacy, exposing sensitive personal details to the public or malicious actors.

- **Economic Impact:** Data breaches and identity theft can lead to significant financial losses, both directly and indirectly, through fraud recovery and reputational damage.

- **Legal and Regulatory Compliance:** Many regions now have strict data protection laws (e.g., GDPR, CCPA) that mandate how personal data should be handled. Protecting your data helps ensure compliance and protects your rights.

7.2 Understanding Your Personal Data

7.2.1 Categories of Personal Data

- **Identifiable Information:** Full name, address, phone number, email address, date of birth.

- **Sensitive Data:** Social security numbers, passport details, financial account information, biometric data.

- **Digital Footprint:** Online activities, browsing history, social media interactions, and location data collected from devices.

- **Health and Medical Records:** Information regarding your physical and mental health, including medical histories and insurance details.

7.2.2 How Data Is Collected

- **Direct Collection:** Data you actively provide when registering for services, filling out forms, or making purchases.

- **Passive Collection:** Data gathered through cookies, tracking pixels, and other technologies as you navigate websites.

- **Third-Party Sharing:** Information collected by one entity and shared with partners or advertisers, often without your explicit consent.

7.3 Common Threats to Personal Data

7.3.1 Data Breaches

- **Definition:** Incidents where unauthorized individuals gain access to a database containing personal information.

- **Impact:** Breaches can lead to exposure of sensitive data, resulting in identity theft, financial loss, and reputational damage.

7.3.2 Phishing and Social Engineering

- **Phishing:** Fraudulent attempts to obtain sensitive information by disguising as a trustworthy entity through emails or messages.

- **Social Engineering:** Manipulative tactics where attackers exploit human behavior to gain confidential information, such as pretexting or baiting.

7.3.3 Tracking and Profiling

- **Online Trackers:** Advertisers and data brokers use cookies, web beacons, and other technologies to track your online activities, building detailed profiles for targeted advertising.

- **Location Data Harvesting:** Apps and devices that constantly collect geolocation data can inadvertently expose your movements and habits.

7.3.4 Malware and Spyware

- **Malware:** Malicious software that can steal data, monitor your activity, or provide a backdoor for attackers.

- **Spyware:** Programs specifically designed to collect information about you without your consent, often operating silently in the background.

7.4 Best Practices for Protecting Your Personal Data

7.4.1 Data Minimization

- **Limit Sharing:** Only provide the minimum required information when signing up for services or completing forms.

- **Review Permissions:** Regularly audit app and website permissions to ensure that only necessary data is being collected.

7.4.2 Secure Storage

- **Encryption:** Use encryption tools to secure data stored on your devices or in the cloud. Encrypt sensitive files and communications to prevent unauthorized access.

- **Access Controls:** Implement strong access controls and authentication methods (e.g., password protection, biometrics) on all devices and accounts.

7.4.3 Regular Monitoring and Auditing

- **Account Activity:** Regularly review the activity logs of your online accounts to detect any unauthorized access.

- **Data Breach Alerts:** Sign up for notifications from services like Have I Been Pwned to stay informed if your data has been compromised.

7.4.4 Safe Data Disposal

- **Data Deletion:** Permanently delete data from devices before disposing of them. Use secure deletion tools that ensure the data cannot be recovered.

- **Shredding Physical Documents:** Shred any physical documents containing sensitive information before discarding them.

7.5 Tools and Technologies for Data Protection

7.5.1 Encryption Tools

- **File and Disk Encryption:** Use tools such as BitLocker (Windows), FileVault (macOS), or VeraCrypt (cross-platform) to encrypt sensitive data.

- **Encrypted Messaging:** Choose communication apps that provide end-to-end encryption, such as Signal or WhatsApp, to protect your conversations.

7.5.2 Virtual Private Networks (VPNs)

- **Secure Browsing:** A reputable VPN encrypts your internet traffic, protecting your data from being intercepted, especially on public or unsecured networks.

- **Privacy Enhancement:** VPNs mask your IP address, making it harder for trackers to build a profile based on your location and browsing habits.

7.5.3 Privacy-Focused Software and Browser Extensions

- **Ad and Tracker Blockers:** Tools like uBlock Origin, Privacy Badger, or Ghostery can help prevent tracking by blocking third-party cookies and trackers.

- **Secure Search Engines:** Consider using privacy-centric search engines (e.g., DuckDuckGo) that do not track your queries or store personal information.

7.5.4 Password Managers and Authentication Tools

- **Password Managers:** As discussed in Chapter 6, password managers not only help you create strong, unique passwords but also secure your credentials using encryption.

- **Multi-Factor Authentication (MFA):** Enabling MFA adds an extra layer of security, ensuring that even if your personal data is compromised, unauthorized access is significantly more difficult.

7.6 Managing Privacy on Social Media and Online Platforms

7.6.1 Reviewing Privacy Settings

- **Profile Visibility:** Regularly review and adjust the privacy settings on your social media accounts to control who can view your posts, personal information, and friend lists.

- **Third-Party Apps:** Limit the number of third-party applications connected to your social media profiles, and revoke permissions for those no longer in use.

7.6.2 Mindful Sharing

- **Oversharing Risks:** Be cautious about the personal details you share publicly. Even seemingly innocuous posts can be used to piece together sensitive information.

- **Geotagging:** Disable geotagging on your posts and photos to avoid revealing your location and routine patterns.

7.6.3 Data Portability and Deletion

- **Exporting Data:** Most platforms allow you to export a copy of your data. Familiarize yourself with these options so you can maintain backups of your personal information.

- **Account Deactivation:** If you no longer use a service, consider deactivating or permanently deleting your account to minimize the data footprint.

7.7 Legal and Regulatory Aspects of Data Privacy

7.7.1 Understanding Data Protection Laws

- **GDPR (General Data Protection Regulation):** A comprehensive set of regulations in the European Union that gives individuals control over their personal data and mandates strict data handling practices for businesses.

- **CCPA (California Consumer Privacy Act):** Provides similar protections for residents of California, including the right to know what personal data is collected and the right to request deletion.

- **Other Regulations:** Be aware of additional regional and national laws that may affect how your data is handled, such as HIPAA for health information in the United States.

7.7.2 Exercising Your Rights

- **Data Access Requests:** Many regulations grant you the right to request access to your personal data from companies. Understand how to exercise these rights and what to expect.

- **Opt-Out Mechanisms:** Take advantage of opt-out options provided by services that allow you to limit the sharing and sale of your personal data.

- **Legal Recourse:** In cases of data misuse or breach, familiarize yourself with the process of filing complaints with regulatory bodies or seeking legal advice.

7.8 Conclusion

Protecting your personal data and privacy is an ongoing process that requires vigilance, education, and the consistent application of best practices. In this chapter, you learned:

- **What Personal Data Is:** A clear definition and understanding of the types of personal information that require protection.

- **Threats to Your Privacy:** An overview of common threats, including data breaches, phishing, and tracking, along with their potential impacts.

- **Practical Protection Strategies:** Detailed best practices for minimizing data collection, securing storage, monitoring account activity, and safely disposing of data.

- **Tools and Technologies:** An exploration of the tools available—such as encryption software, VPNs, and privacy-focused browser extensions—that can help safeguard your information.

- **Social Media Management:** How to adjust privacy settings, limit oversharing, and manage connected apps on social platforms.

- **Legal Protections:** An introduction to the regulatory frameworks designed to protect your data rights and how to exercise those rights.

By applying these strategies and using the tools provided, you can significantly reduce your exposure to data breaches, identity theft, and privacy invasions. Remember that protecting your personal data is not a one-time effort but a continuous commitment to monitoring, updating, and refining your privacy practices in an ever-evolving digital landscape.

As you progress further into this guide, keep in mind that the steps you take to protect your personal information will not only secure your digital life but also empower you to confidently navigate the interconnected world.

Chapter 8: Social Media and Your Digital Footprint

Social media platforms have revolutionized the way we communicate, share, and connect. However, with this connectivity comes the challenge of managing your digital footprint—a trail of data you leave behind with every post, like, and share. This chapter delves into how social media can both enrich your life and expose you to risks, and it offers a complete, detailed guide on managing your digital identity while balancing connectivity with privacy.

8.1 Introduction to Social Media and Digital Footprints

8.1.1 What Is a Digital Footprint?

Your digital footprint is the collection of all the data you generate online. This includes:

- **Active Footprints:** Content you deliberately share, such as posts, photos, comments, and videos.

- **Passive Footprints:** Data collected without your direct input, like browsing histories, likes, geolocation data, and metadata attached to your uploads.

8.1.2 The Role of Social Media

Social media platforms—such as Facebook, Instagram, Twitter, LinkedIn, and TikTok—provide powerful tools for personal expression, networking, and business. However, every interaction on these platforms adds to your digital footprint, influencing:

- **Privacy:** The amount of personal information visible to others.

- **Reputation:** How you are perceived by employers, friends, and the public.

- **Security:** How easily cybercriminals can exploit personal information.

8.1.3 The Dual Nature of Social Media

While social media offers connectivity and access to a global audience, it also poses risks:

- **Exposure:** Unintended sharing of sensitive information can lead to identity theft or stalking.

- **Manipulation:** Data can be used to target you with personalized scams or misleading information.

- **Permanent Records:** Once information is online, it can be challenging to fully remove—even with privacy settings adjusted later.

8.2 Risks Associated with Social Media

8.2.1 Privacy Invasions

- **Oversharing:** Posting details such as your location, daily routines, or personal milestones can reveal more than you intend.

- **Third-Party Data Collection:** Social media platforms and connected apps often collect and share data with advertisers or data brokers without your explicit awareness.

- **Geotagging:** Including location data in posts or photos can disclose your current or frequent whereabouts.

8.2.2 Social Engineering and Cyber Threats

- **Phishing and Scams:** Cybercriminals may impersonate friends or trusted brands to trick you into revealing login credentials or financial information.

- **Impersonation:** Fake profiles and identity theft can damage your reputation or be used to commit fraud.

- **Malicious Links:** Posts and direct messages can contain harmful links that install malware or lead to fraudulent sites.

8.2.3 Reputation and Professional Risks

- **Employer Scrutiny:** Content you post may be viewed by potential or current employers, affecting your professional reputation.

- **Permanent Records:** Even deleted posts can be archived or screenshotted, creating a lasting digital record.

- **Context Collapse:** Personal posts intended for a small group can be viewed by a broader, unintended audience, leading to misunderstandings.

8.3 Managing Your Digital Identity

8.3.1 Understanding and Auditing Your Profiles

- **Review Your Accounts:** Regularly review the privacy settings and content of all your social media profiles.

- **Search Yourself:** Perform searches of your name on various platforms and search engines to see what information is publicly available.

- **Clean Up Old Content:** Remove or archive posts, photos, and comments that no longer represent your current identity or that reveal sensitive information.

8.3.2 Privacy Settings and Account Controls

- **Adjust Privacy Options:** Use platform-specific privacy controls to restrict who can see your content, friend lists, and personal details.

- **Custom Audiences:** On platforms like Facebook, customize audience settings to share posts with only selected groups.

- **Two-Factor Authentication (2FA):** Enable 2FA on your social media accounts to add an extra layer of protection.

8.3.3 Controlling Third-Party Access

- **Review App Permissions:** Periodically audit the list of third-party apps connected to your accounts and remove those you no longer use.

- **Limit Data Sharing:** Adjust settings to minimize data sharing with advertisers and external websites.

- **Opt-Out Options:** Where possible, opt out of data collection practices and targeted advertising programs.

8.4 Best Practices for Social Media Safety

8.4.1 Think Before You Share

- **Evaluate Content:** Before posting, consider whether the information could be misused or harm your reputation.

- **Delay Posting:** Taking a moment to reflect on the content you're about to share can help avoid impulsive oversharing.

- **Educate Yourself:** Understand the privacy policies and data practices of each platform you use.

8.4.2 Secure Communication on Social Platforms

- **Verify Contacts:** Only accept friend or follower requests from people you know, and be cautious with unsolicited messages.

- **Avoid Sensitive Topics:** Refrain from sharing sensitive personal details (e.g., financial information, home address) in public posts or comments.

- **Report Suspicious Activity:** Utilize built-in reporting tools to flag phishing attempts, impersonation, or other malicious behaviors.

8.4.3 Digital Etiquette and Mindful Engagement

- **Be Respectful:** Maintain a professional and respectful tone online to protect your reputation.

- **Separate Personal and Professional:** Consider using separate accounts for personal interactions and professional networking.

- **Monitor Engagement:** Regularly check and moderate comments and interactions on your posts to prevent harassment or unwanted attention.

8.5 Tools and Techniques to Monitor and Manage Your Digital Footprint

8.5.1 Social Media Monitoring Tools

- **Reputation Management Services:** Use services like Google Alerts or specialized reputation management tools to monitor mentions of your name online.

- **Privacy Audit Tools:** Some platforms offer tools to review your privacy settings or help audit your digital footprint across multiple services.

- **Browser Extensions:** Utilize extensions that can block trackers and alert you to privacy concerns while browsing social media sites.

8.5.2 Content Scheduling and Management Tools

- **Content Calendars:** Plan your posts in advance to ensure that content aligns with your privacy and professional goals.

- **Analytics Tools:** Use analytics to monitor who is engaging with your content and adjust your privacy settings accordingly.

8.5.3 Data Removal and Account Recovery Services

- **Data Deletion Requests:** Learn how to request the deletion of personal data from platforms or search engines.

- **Account Recovery:** Familiarize yourself with the process for recovering compromised or hacked accounts, including the use of 2FA and backup emails.

8.6 Balancing Connectivity with Privacy

8.6.1 Creating a Personal Social Media Strategy

- **Define Your Goals:** Determine what you want to achieve through social media—be it personal expression, professional networking, or staying informed—and tailor your privacy settings accordingly.

- **Set Boundaries:** Decide in advance what personal information you are willing to share and what should remain private.

- **Regular Reviews:** Schedule periodic reviews of your social media presence to ensure it still aligns with your current personal and professional goals.

8.6.2 Educating Your Network

- **Promote Digital Literacy:** Encourage friends and family to adopt similar privacy practices.

- **Share Best Practices:** If you manage a business or community page, share guidelines on safe social media usage.

- **Stay Informed:** Keep up with evolving privacy features and best practices on social media platforms, and update your settings as needed.

8.6.3 Leveraging Privacy-Enhancing Features

- **Anonymous or Pseudonymous Accounts:** Consider using pseudonyms for certain interactions to maintain a level of anonymity.

- **Temporary Sharing Options:** Use features like Instagram or Snapchat stories, which disappear after a set period, for sharing more personal moments.

- **Selective Sharing:** Use private groups or direct messaging for conversations that require greater privacy.

8.7 Real-World Examples and Case Studies

8.7.1 Oversharing and Its Consequences

- **Case Study – Identity Theft:** An individual who shared too many details about their daily routine and location on social media became a target for identity thieves. The attackers used this information to access sensitive accounts and commit fraud.

- **Lessons Learned:** Regularly audit the type of content you share and adjust privacy settings to limit exposure.

8.7.2 Professional Repercussions

- **Case Study – Social Media Missteps:** A professional faced repercussions when a casual post was misinterpreted by a prospective employer. The incident highlights the importance of separating personal opinions from professional branding.

- **Lessons Learned:** Consider using separate accounts for professional and personal use, and be mindful of the long-term implications of online posts.

8.7.3 Positive Uses of Digital Footprint Management

- **Case Study – Reputation Repair:** An individual successfully managed their digital footprint by proactively deleting outdated content and enhancing privacy settings after a data breach. Their efforts led to restored personal and professional relationships.

- **Lessons Learned:** It's never too late to clean up your digital footprint; proactive management can help repair and even enhance your online reputation.

8.8 Conclusion

Managing your digital footprint on social media is an ongoing process that requires vigilance, education, and strategic planning. In this chapter, you learned:

- **The Definition and Impact:** What constitutes your digital footprint and why it matters for both privacy and reputation.

- **Risks on Social Media:** How oversharing, third-party data collection, and cyber threats can compromise your privacy.

- **Managing Your Identity:** Practical steps to audit and adjust your online profiles, use privacy settings effectively, and control third-party access.

- **Best Practices:** Strategies for secure engagement on social media, including thoughtful sharing, account security measures, and proactive reputation management.

- **Tools and Techniques:** Various monitoring, content management, and data removal tools available to help you maintain control over your digital presence.

- **Balancing Act:** How to achieve the right balance between staying connected and protecting your privacy, with real-world examples illustrating both pitfalls and successful strategies.

By applying these guidelines and continually reviewing your social media practices, you can enjoy the benefits of digital connectivity while maintaining a secure and controlled online presence. As you move forward, remember that your digital footprint is a living record— one that you can shape and protect through informed choices and ongoing vigilance.

Chapter 9: Cybersecurity for Small Businesses

Small businesses are the backbone of many economies, yet they often face significant cybersecurity challenges despite limited resources. This chapter provides a detailed guide for small business owners and managers, outlining the unique risks they face, practical strategies to mitigate those risks, and a roadmap for building a robust cybersecurity posture without requiring a large IT department or extensive technical expertise.

9.1 The Unique Cybersecurity Landscape for Small Businesses

9.1.1 Understanding the Threat Environment

Small businesses are frequently perceived as easy targets by cybercriminals due to:

- **Limited Security Budgets:** Many small enterprises lack the financial and human resources dedicated to cybersecurity.

- **Outdated Infrastructure:** Older systems and software can leave businesses exposed to known vulnerabilities.

- **Underdeveloped Policies:** Without comprehensive security policies, employees may inadvertently expose sensitive information.

- **Interconnected Operations:** The integration of digital tools—such as cloud services, payment systems, and remote work solutions—expands the potential attack surface.

9.1.2 Common Threats Targeting Small Businesses

- **Phishing and Social Engineering:** Employees may be tricked into revealing login credentials or installing malware through deceptive emails or phone calls.

- **Ransomware:** A single successful ransomware attack can halt operations, encrypt critical business files, and demand significant ransom payments.

- **Data Breaches:** Unsecured customer data, financial records, and proprietary information can be compromised, leading to legal liabilities and loss of trust.

- **Insider Threats:** Whether intentional or accidental, employees with access to sensitive data can become a risk factor.

- **Third-Party Vulnerabilities:** Vendors or partners with inadequate security can become conduits for cyberattacks.

9.2 Building a Foundation for Cybersecurity

9.2.1 Establishing a Security Mindset

- **Risk Awareness:** Recognize that every digital asset—no matter how small—requires protection.

- **Proactive Attitude:** Understand that cybersecurity is not a one-time project but a continuous effort that evolves with emerging threats.

- **Ownership:** Ensure that cybersecurity is integrated into the business culture, with clear roles and responsibilities defined across the organization.

9.2.2 Assessing Your Current Security Posture

- **Security Audit:** Conduct a thorough review of your current systems, software, and policies to identify vulnerabilities.

- **Asset Inventory:** Document all hardware, software, and data repositories to know what needs protection.

- **Threat Modeling:** Identify potential attackers and attack vectors that might target your business operations.

9.2.3 Setting Cybersecurity Goals and Policies

- **Define Objectives:** Establish what you need to protect (e.g., customer data, financial records, intellectual property) and set measurable security goals.

- **Develop Policies:** Create clear guidelines on password management, data handling, software updates, and employee conduct.

- **Compliance:** Ensure that your policies align with relevant data protection laws (e.g., GDPR, CCPA) and industry standards.

9.3 Essential Cybersecurity Tools and Strategies

9.3.1 Hardware and Network Security

- **Firewalls:** Install and configure both software and hardware firewalls to control incoming and outgoing network traffic.

- **Router Security:** Update router firmware regularly, change default credentials, and segment your network to isolate critical systems.

- **Secure Wi-Fi:** Use strong encryption (WPA3, if available) for wireless networks and restrict access to authorized devices only.

9.3.2 Software and System Protection

- **Regular Updates and Patches:** Ensure that all operating systems, applications, and devices are updated regularly to patch known vulnerabilities.

- **Antivirus/Anti-Malware Software:** Deploy reputable antivirus and anti-malware solutions that provide real-time scanning and threat detection.

- **Backup Solutions:** Implement automated, regular backups of critical data. Store backups securely off-site or in a reputable cloud service with encryption.

- **Encryption:** Use encryption tools to protect sensitive data both at rest and during transmission.

9.3.3 Secure Cloud Practices

- **Vendor Evaluation:** Choose cloud service providers with strong security reputations and certifications.

- **Access Controls:** Implement strict access controls for cloud services, ensuring that only authorized personnel can access sensitive data.

- **Data Encryption:** Ensure that data stored in the cloud is encrypted and that you understand the vendor's policies on data protection.

9.4 Employee Training and Security Policies

9.4.1 Cultivating a Security-Aware Culture

- **Regular Training:** Provide regular cybersecurity awareness training to all employees, covering topics such as phishing, social engineering, and secure data handling.

- **Clear Communication:** Ensure that employees understand the importance of following security policies and know whom to contact if they suspect a breach.

- **Role-Based Training:** Tailor training programs to the specific needs of different roles within the organization—from administrative staff to technical personnel.

9.4.2 Implementing Robust Policies and Procedures

- **Access Management:** Establish strict protocols for account creation, password management, and multi-factor authentication.

- **Incident Reporting:** Develop and communicate clear procedures for reporting suspicious activity or security incidents.

- **Data Handling:** Define guidelines for the storage, transmission, and disposal of sensitive information.

- **Vendor Management:** Set standards for evaluating the cybersecurity practices of third-party vendors and partners.

9.5 Incident Response and Business Continuity Planning

9.5.1 Developing an Incident Response Plan

- **Preparation:** Establish an incident response team with defined roles and responsibilities.

- **Identification:** Implement systems to detect anomalies and potential breaches early.

- **Containment and Eradication:** Develop step-by-step procedures for isolating compromised systems and removing threats.

- **Recovery:** Plan for the rapid restoration of systems and data to minimize downtime and financial impact.

- **Post-Incident Analysis:** After an incident, review the response to identify lessons learned and improve future protocols.

9.5.2 Business Continuity Strategies

- **Redundancy:** Invest in redundant systems and backup communication channels to maintain operations during a crisis.

- **Regular Drills:** Conduct periodic drills to test the effectiveness of your incident response and business continuity plans.

- **Insurance:** Consider cybersecurity insurance as a financial safeguard against the costs associated with data breaches and other cyber incidents.

9.6 Leveraging External Resources and Expertise

9.6.1 Working with Managed Service Providers (MSPs)

- **Outsourced Expertise:** For businesses lacking in-house expertise, partnering with an MSP can provide ongoing monitoring, maintenance, and incident response.

- **Cost-Effective Solutions:** MSPs offer scalable security services tailored to small businesses, ensuring professional support without the expense of a full IT department.

9.6.2 Utilizing Government and Industry Resources

- **Cybersecurity Frameworks:** Leverage resources such as the NIST Cybersecurity Framework to guide your security efforts.

- **Local and National Programs:** Many governments and industry organizations offer free or low-cost cybersecurity tools, training, and consultation services targeted at small businesses.

- **Peer Networks:** Join local business associations or online communities to share best practices and learn from the experiences of other small business owners.

9.7 Conclusion

Cybersecurity is a critical consideration for small businesses, where the impact of an attack can be disproportionately high compared to larger organizations. In this chapter, you have learned:

- **Unique Risks:** The specific challenges small businesses face in the cybersecurity landscape.

- **Foundation Building:** How to establish a security-first culture through assessments, policies, and clear objectives.

- **Practical Tools:** Essential hardware, software, and cloud-based strategies to safeguard your business operations.

- **Employee Engagement:** The importance of training and clear procedures in reducing human error and insider threats.

- **Incident Preparedness:** Steps for developing effective incident response and business continuity plans.

- **External Support:** Ways to leverage managed service providers and public resources for enhanced protection.

By adopting these strategies and continuously adapting to the evolving threat environment, small businesses can build resilient defenses and secure their operations against the cyber threats of today and tomorrow. Cybersecurity is not just a technical requirement—it is an integral part of safeguarding your business's reputation, assets, and future growth.

As you move forward, remember that the journey to robust cybersecurity is ongoing. Regular reviews, updates, and training are essential to maintaining a secure environment in a rapidly changing digital world.

Chapter 10: Mobile Security: Protecting Your On-the-Go Devices

Mobile devices—smartphones and tablets—have become indispensable tools in our daily lives, enabling communication, work, entertainment, and much more. However, their portability and constant connectivity also make them attractive targets for cybercriminals. This chapter provides a detailed, step-by-step guide to securing your mobile devices, covering topics from operating system updates to secure communications and safe app management. Whether you use Android, iOS, or another mobile platform, the following strategies will help protect your sensitive data and preserve your privacy while you're on the go.

10.1 Introduction to Mobile Security

10.1.1 The Importance of Mobile Security

- **Data on the Move:** Mobile devices store and transmit vast amounts of personal and professional data, making them valuable targets for attackers.

- **Portability and Exposure:** Unlike stationary computers, mobile devices are constantly in use—across various networks and locations—exposing them to a broader range of threats.

- **Integrated Functionality:** Modern smartphones

and tablets often integrate multiple functionalities (e.g., email, banking, social media), meaning a breach on one app can have wide-reaching implications.

10.1.2 The Evolving Threat Landscape for Mobile Devices

- **Malware and Spyware:** Malicious apps and hidden software can infect your device to steal information, track your location, or even control device functions remotely.

- **Phishing and Smishing:** Mobile users are targeted with phishing (fraudulent emails) and smishing (phishing via SMS) attacks designed to capture credentials or install malicious software.

- **Network Attacks:** Public Wi-Fi and insecure cellular networks can be exploited by attackers to intercept data or inject malicious code.

- **Physical Theft or Loss:** A lost or stolen device can provide an attacker with direct access to your data if adequate security measures are not in place.

10.2 Understanding Mobile Threats

10.2.1 Mobile Malware and Ransomware

- **Definition:** Mobile malware is software designed to infiltrate your device, steal sensitive data, or hijack its functionality. Ransomware on mobile devices can lock you out of critical apps or encrypt files, demanding a ransom for restoration.

- **Delivery Mechanisms:** Malware often spreads through malicious apps, compromised app stores, or deceptive links in messages and emails.

10.2.2 Phishing, Smishing, and Social Engineering

- **Phishing:** Fraudulent emails or messages that mimic trusted sources, urging you to click on links or provide personal details.

- **Smishing:** Similar to phishing, but delivered via SMS, where attackers use text messages to lure you into divulging sensitive information.

- **Social Engineering:** Tactics that exploit human psychology—such as urgency or trust—to trick you into compromising security, for example by installing unauthorized apps or revealing login credentials.

10.2.3 App and OS Vulnerabilities

- **Unpatched Software:** Outdated operating systems and apps may have unpatched vulnerabilities that attackers can exploit.

- **Malicious Apps:** Some apps, especially those downloaded from unofficial sources, may contain hidden malware or request unnecessary permissions.

- **Inter-App Exploits:** Vulnerabilities in how apps interact can be exploited to gain unauthorized access to data stored on your device.

10.3 Securing Your Mobile Operating System and Apps

10.3.1 Keep Your Operating System Updated

- **Automatic Updates:** Enable automatic updates for your mobile OS to ensure that you receive the latest security patches as soon as they are released.

- **Regular Checks:** Periodically check for OS updates manually, especially if automatic updates are disabled due to data concerns.

10.3.2 Manage App Installations Carefully

- **Official App Stores:** Only download apps from reputable sources like the Apple App Store or Google Play Store, as these platforms employ security screening processes.

- **Review Permissions:** Scrutinize the permissions requested by an app before installation. Avoid apps that request access to sensitive data or functions that aren't necessary for their operation.

- **Update Apps Regularly:** Ensure that all installed apps are up to date, as developers often release patches to fix security vulnerabilities.

10.3.3 Use Security Software on Mobile Devices

- **Mobile Antivirus:** Consider installing a trusted antivirus or mobile security app that offers real-time protection, malware scanning, and safe browsing features.

- **App Scanners:** Some security apps can analyze installed applications for suspicious behavior or excessive permissions.

10.4 Best Practices for Mobile Device Management

10.4.1 Secure Device Settings

- **Strong Lock Screen:** Use a robust lock screen method such as a strong PIN, complex password, or biometric authentication (fingerprint or facial recognition).

- **Auto-Lock Feature:** Set your device to auto-lock after a short period of inactivity to minimize the window of opportunity for unauthorized access.

- **Disable Unnecessary Features:** Turn off features like Bluetooth, NFC, or location services when not in use to reduce potential entry points for attackers.

10.4.2 Encrypt Your Mobile Data

- **Full-Disk Encryption:** Most modern mobile devices offer encryption that protects the data stored on your device. Ensure that this feature is enabled in your device settings.

- **Encrypted Communications:** Use apps that offer end-to-end encryption for messaging, calls, and file transfers, ensuring your communications remain private.

10.4.3 Backup Your Data Regularly

- **Cloud Backups:** Use encrypted cloud backup services to store copies of your data securely. This is critical in case your device is lost, stolen, or compromised.

- **Local Backups:** In addition to cloud backups, consider periodic local backups to a secure computer or external storage device, ensuring you can restore your data if needed.

10.5 Securing Mobile Communications

10.5.1 Use a Virtual Private Network (VPN)

- **Public Wi-Fi Safety:** Always use a reputable VPN when connecting to public Wi-Fi networks. This encrypts your data and protects it from interception.

- **Reliable VPN Services:** Choose a VPN service with strong encryption standards, a no-logs policy, and positive user reviews to ensure maximum protection.

10.5.2 Secure Messaging and Email

- **Encrypted Apps:** Opt for messaging apps that provide end-to-end encryption (e.g., Signal, WhatsApp) to secure your conversations.

- **Secure Email Providers:** Consider using email services that prioritize security and privacy, offering features such as encrypted emails and two-factor authentication.

10.5.3 Protect Against Phishing and Smishing

- **Vigilance:** Be cautious of unsolicited messages and emails that request personal information or urge you to click on unfamiliar links.

- **Verification:** Verify the authenticity of any unexpected message by contacting the sender through a known, trusted channel before taking action.

- **Spam Filters:** Use and regularly update spam filters provided by your email or messaging service to reduce the risk of phishing attempts.

10.6 Safe Use of Public Networks and Mobile Connectivity

10.6.1 Public Wi-Fi and Hotspot Caution

- **Avoid Sensitive Transactions:** Refrain from accessing sensitive accounts (e.g., banking, email) over public Wi-Fi unless using a VPN.

- **Personal Hotspots:** When possible, use your device's personal hotspot feature instead of public networks to maintain greater control over your connection security.

10.6.2 Cellular Data Security

- **Data Encryption:** Cellular networks are generally more secure than public Wi-Fi, but ensure that your device settings enforce encryption for data communications.

- **Monitor Data Usage:** Keep an eye on your data usage for any unusual spikes, which could indicate that your device is transmitting data without your consent.

10.7 Mobile Device Recovery and Remote Management

10.7.1 Enable Remote Tracking and Wiping

- **Find My Device:** Activate services like "Find My iPhone" (iOS) or "Find My Device" (Android) to locate your device if it's lost or stolen.

- **Remote Wipe:** Ensure that remote wipe capabilities are enabled so you can erase sensitive data from your device if it falls into the wrong hands.

10.7.2 Maintain an Inventory of Devices

- **Device Records:** Keep a record of all your mobile devices, including serial numbers and other identifying information. This can help in recovery efforts and when reporting a lost device.

- **Regular Audits:** Periodically review your list of devices and ensure that security settings and recovery features are up to date on each one.

10.8 Conclusion

Mobile security is an essential component of your overall cybersecurity strategy, especially as our lives become increasingly intertwined with our portable devices. In this chapter, you have learned:

- **The Importance of Mobile Security:** Understanding why mobile devices are attractive targets and the types of threats they face.

- **Threat Landscape:** An in-depth look at mobile malware, phishing, and vulnerabilities that can compromise your device.

- **Securing the OS and Apps:** Best practices for keeping your mobile operating system and applications up to date and secure.

- **Device Management:** Key measures such as strong lock screens, encryption, and regular backups to safeguard your data.

- **Secure Communications:** The role of VPNs, encrypted messaging, and cautious use of public networks in protecting your mobile data.

- **Recovery Strategies:** How to enable remote tracking and wiping, and the importance of maintaining an inventory of your devices.

By implementing these strategies and remaining vigilant, you can significantly reduce the risk of compromise on your mobile devices. The convenience of mobile technology should not come at the cost of security—by adopting these best practices, you are better equipped to navigate the digital landscape safely, ensuring that your personal data and communications remain secure while on the go.

With mobile security in place, you are now ready to further explore the evolving landscape of cybersecurity in specialized contexts. In the next chapters, we will delve into how to respond to cyber incidents and prepare for the future of digital threats, ensuring that every aspect of your digital life is robustly protected.

Chapter 11: Responding to Cyber Incidents

Even with robust preventive measures, no system is entirely immune to cyber attacks. Responding effectively to a cyber incident is critical in mitigating damage, recovering operations, and preventing future occurrences. This chapter provides a detailed, step-by-step guide to recognizing, managing, and recovering from cyber incidents. It covers everything from identifying early warning signs to post-incident analysis and continuous improvement, ensuring that whether you're an individual user or a small business owner, you're equipped to handle crises swiftly and decisively.

11.1 Introduction to Cyber Incident Response

11.1.1 The Importance of a Proactive Response

- **Rapid Mitigation:** Quick detection and response can significantly reduce the impact of an incident.

- **Minimizing Damage:** Effective response strategies limit data loss, financial impact, and reputational damage.

- **Regulatory Compliance:** Many data protection laws require timely reporting and remediation in the event of a breach.

- **Continuous Improvement:** Post-incident analysis provides critical insights to improve future defenses.

11.1.2 Defining a Cyber Incident

- **Cyber Incident:** Any event that results in unauthorized access, damage, or disruption to digital systems, data, or services. Examples include malware infections, data breaches, ransomware attacks, and DDoS events.

- **Incident vs. Breach:** While all breaches are incidents, not all incidents result in a data breach. An incident can also be a thwarted attack or an attempted compromise.

11.2 Identifying Cyber Incidents

11.2.1 Recognizing the Warning Signs

- **Unusual Activity:** Unexpected changes in system performance, unexplained network traffic spikes, or frequent system crashes.

- **Unauthorized Access:** Alerts from intrusion detection systems (IDS), unusual login attempts, or unfamiliar user activities.

- **Data Irregularities:** Sudden changes in data integrity, unexplained data deletion, or unauthorized modifications.

- **User Reports:** Feedback from employees, customers, or IT staff noticing suspicious emails, pop-ups, or anomalies in system behavior.

11.2.2 Tools for Detection

- **Intrusion Detection/Prevention Systems (IDS/IPS):** Monitor network traffic and system behavior for signs of intrusion.

- **Security Information and Event Management (SIEM) Systems:** Aggregate and analyze log data from various sources to detect anomalies.

- **Endpoint Detection and Response (EDR):** Provides continuous monitoring and response capabilities on individual devices.

- **Automated Alerts:** Configure software and systems to send real-time alerts when predefined security thresholds are exceeded.

11.3 Incident Response Planning

11.3.1 Developing an Incident Response Plan (IRP)

- **Establishing a Team:** Designate an incident response team with clearly defined roles and responsibilities. This team may include IT staff, legal advisors, PR personnel, and external experts.

- **Defining Procedures:** Outline step-by-step processes for identification, containment, eradication, and recovery. Create flowcharts and checklists to ensure clarity and consistency.

- **Communication Protocols:** Develop internal and external communication strategies, including how to report incidents, who to contact, and guidelines for public disclosure.

- **Resource Allocation:** Identify and allocate necessary resources such as backup systems, forensic tools, and external cybersecurity partners.

- **Regular Training:** Conduct training sessions and simulation exercises (tabletop exercises or full-scale drills) to ensure that all team members are familiar with the plan.

11.3.2 Establishing Incident Categories and Severity Levels

- **Incident Categorization:** Define what constitutes a minor incident, a moderate incident, and a major incident based on the potential impact on operations and data.

- **Severity Levels:** Develop criteria to assess the severity of an incident, taking into account factors like data sensitivity, affected systems, and potential financial loss.

- **Response Triggers:** Establish clear thresholds that trigger specific response actions, ensuring that the team can act swiftly and in proportion to the threat.

11.4 Containment, Eradication, and Recovery

11.4.1 Containment Strategies

- **Immediate Isolation:** Isolate affected systems or networks to prevent the spread of the incident. This might involve disconnecting systems from the network, blocking IP addresses, or shutting down compromised servers.

- **Short-Term vs. Long-Term Containment:**

    o **Short-Term:** Stop the immediate threat by halting ongoing malicious activity.

    o **Long-Term:** Implement changes to prevent the attacker from re-entering the system, such as patching vulnerabilities or changing access controls.

- **Document Actions:** Keep detailed records of all containment measures taken for later analysis and reporting.

11.4.2 Eradication Techniques

- **Removing Threats:** Identify and remove malware, unauthorized software, or malicious code from affected systems.

- **Patching Vulnerabilities:** Update software, install security patches, and correct misconfigurations that allowed the incident.

- **Credential Resets:** Reset passwords and update authentication mechanisms for compromised accounts.

- **System Scanning:** Use antivirus, anti-malware, and forensic tools to ensure that the threat has been fully eradicated.

11.4.3 Recovery Processes

- **Restoration from Backups:** Restore systems and data from verified, secure backups. Ensure that backups are clean and uninfected before reintroducing them to the network.

- **System Testing:** Perform thorough testing of restored systems to verify that they are functioning correctly and securely.

- **Monitoring:** Increase monitoring efforts post-recovery to detect any signs of residual or recurring threats.

- **Gradual Reconnection:** Reconnect systems to the network gradually and monitor their behavior closely during the reintegration process.

11.5 Reporting and Communication

11.5.1 Internal Reporting

- **Incident Log:** Maintain a comprehensive log of all actions taken, observations made, and communications exchanged during the incident.

- **Team Debrief:** Conduct an immediate debrief with the incident response team to review the incident, assess the effectiveness of the response, and document lessons learned.

11.5.2 External Reporting

- **Regulatory Bodies:** If required by law or industry standards, report the incident to relevant authorities (e.g., data protection authorities, law enforcement).

- **Stakeholder Communication:** Inform affected stakeholders—such as customers, partners, and employees—about the incident, what data may have been compromised, and the steps being taken to remediate the situation.

- **Public Relations:** Develop a clear and honest public statement if the incident has significant public impact, balancing transparency with the need to protect sensitive details that could aid further attacks.

11.6 Post-Incident Analysis and Continuous Improvement

11.6.1 Conducting a Post-Mortem

- **Root Cause Analysis:** Determine the underlying cause of the incident, including vulnerabilities or lapses in procedures that were exploited.

- **Effectiveness Assessment:** Evaluate how well the incident response plan performed. Identify strengths to build on and weaknesses to address.

- **Documentation:** Compile a detailed report that includes a timeline of events, actions taken, outcomes, and recommendations for improvement.

11.6.2 Updating Policies and Procedures

- **Plan Revision:** Based on the post-mortem findings, update the incident response plan to address any deficiencies and incorporate new lessons learned.

- **Training Updates:** Modify training programs to include insights from the incident, ensuring that the team is better prepared for future events.

- **Regular Reviews:** Schedule periodic reviews of incident response procedures to keep them current with evolving threats and technologies.

11.7 Conclusion

Responding effectively to cyber incidents is as critical as preventing them. In this chapter, you have learned:

- **The Importance of Preparedness:** How a well-crafted incident response plan can minimize damage and reduce recovery time.

- **Detection and Identification:** The warning signs of cyber incidents and the tools available to identify them promptly.

- **Actionable Steps:** Detailed processes for containment, eradication, and recovery to restore systems and safeguard data.

- **Communication Strategies:** Best practices for internal and external reporting to ensure transparency and regulatory compliance.

- **Continuous Improvement:** The value of post-incident analysis to learn from each event and enhance your security posture.

By integrating these strategies into your overall cybersecurity framework, you can respond to incidents swiftly and effectively, minimizing their impact and reinforcing your defenses against future threats. Remember, a proactive and well-practiced incident response is essential in today's dynamic digital landscape.

As you prepare for the next steps in securing your digital environment, keep in mind that every incident is an opportunity to learn and improve. The resilience of your cybersecurity strategy is built on continuous vigilance, adaptation, and a commitment to best practices.

Chapter 12: The Future of Cybersecurity: Emerging Trends and Technologies

As the digital landscape continues to evolve, so too does the field of cybersecurity. New technologies, shifting threat paradigms, and global trends are redefining what it means to protect digital assets. In this chapter, we explore the emerging trends and technologies that are shaping the future of cybersecurity. By understanding these developments, you can better prepare for tomorrow's challenges and take proactive steps to safeguard your digital environment.

12.1 Introduction: Looking Toward Tomorrow

Cybersecurity is no longer a static discipline—it is a dynamic field driven by constant innovation and ever-changing threat landscapes. In this opening section, we examine the need to anticipate future threats, embrace emerging technologies, and adapt security strategies accordingly.

- **Rapid Technological Advancements:** Innovations in areas such as artificial intelligence (AI), machine learning (ML), and quantum computing are transforming both cyberattack techniques and defense mechanisms.

- **Evolving Threat Vectors:** Cybercriminals are continually refining their methods, targeting new vulnerabilities in interconnected devices, cloud services, and critical infrastructure.

- **Global Digital Transformation:** The rise of remote work, increased reliance on cloud computing, and the proliferation of Internet of Things (IoT) devices are all driving changes in the cybersecurity landscape.

Understanding these trends is essential for developing adaptive strategies that can meet future challenges head-on.

12.2 Emerging Threats on the Horizon

Cyber threats are evolving at an unprecedented pace, leveraging advanced technologies and sophisticated tactics to breach even the most robust defenses. This section highlights key emerging threats:

12.2.1 Advanced AI-Powered Attacks

- **Automated Attack Systems:** Cybercriminals are increasingly using AI and ML to automate attacks, allowing them to scan networks for vulnerabilities, generate polymorphic malware, and adapt tactics in real time.

- **Deepfakes and Social Engineering:** Advances in AI-generated content can produce convincing deepfakes and manipulated media, making it harder to distinguish legitimate communications from fraudulent ones.

12.2.2 Quantum Computing Risks

- **Breaking Encryption:** Quantum computers hold the potential to break traditional encryption methods by performing calculations that are currently infeasible for classical computers. This poses a significant risk to data protection protocols.

- **Quantum-Resistant Algorithms:** The development of quantum-safe cryptography is underway to counter these threats, but widespread adoption will take time and careful integration.

12.2.3 IoT and Edge Computing Vulnerabilities

- **Proliferation of IoT Devices:** As more devices become interconnected—from smart home appliances to industrial control systems—the attack surface expands. Many IoT devices lack robust security features.

- **Edge Computing Challenges:** Distributed computing at the network edge creates new points of vulnerability, requiring innovative strategies to secure data processing outside centralized data centers.

12.2.4 Supply Chain and Third-Party Risks

- **Complex Ecosystems:** Cyber attackers are increasingly targeting supply chains and third-party vendors, knowing that a breach in one weak link can compromise an entire network.

- **Interconnected Services:** The reliance on third-party services and cloud platforms necessitates enhanced scrutiny and robust vendor risk management practices.

12.3 Emerging Technologies in Cybersecurity

Advancements in technology are not only contributing to new threats—they are also equipping defenders with powerful tools to combat them. Here we explore some key innovations:

12.3.1 Artificial Intelligence and Machine Learning

- **Threat Detection and Response:** AI and ML are being used to analyze vast amounts of data, identify anomalies, and predict potential threats before they cause harm. These systems can adapt to new patterns and provide near-real-time insights.

- **Behavioral Analytics:** By monitoring user behavior, AI can help detect deviations from normal patterns that might indicate a compromised account or insider threat.

12.3.2 Quantum-Safe Cryptography

- **Next-Generation Encryption:** As quantum computing advances, researchers are developing cryptographic algorithms that can withstand quantum attacks. Transitioning to quantum-resistant methods will be critical for future data protection.

- **Hybrid Approaches:** Combining classical and quantum-resistant encryption techniques may offer transitional solutions as the industry shifts toward new standards.

12.3.3 Blockchain and Distributed Ledger Technology

- **Decentralized Security:** Blockchain technology offers a decentralized and tamper-resistant method for securing transactions and data exchanges. This can enhance the integrity of supply chains and digital identities.

- **Smart Contracts:** Self-executing contracts stored on the blockchain can automate and enforce security policies, reducing the risk of human error and increasing transparency.

12.3.4 Zero Trust Architecture

- **Never Trust, Always Verify:** The zero trust model assumes that no entity, whether inside or outside the network, can be trusted by default. This approach enforces strict identity verification and microsegmentation.

- **Adaptive Security:** Zero trust architectures continuously monitor and assess every access request, ensuring that security policies dynamically adjust based on risk levels.

12.3.5 Automation and Orchestration

- **Streamlined Response:** Security automation and orchestration (SAO) tools integrate various security functions, enabling faster incident detection, response, and remediation.

- **Reducing Human Error:** By automating routine tasks and standardizing responses, organizations can reduce the risk of mistakes during high-pressure situations.

12.4 Future Trends in Cybersecurity Practices

Anticipating future challenges requires not only adopting new technologies but also evolving the practices and philosophies that underpin cybersecurity. Key trends include:

12.4.1 Increased Focus on Privacy-Enhancing Technologies

- **Data Minimization:** Organizations will place greater emphasis on collecting only the necessary data and using anonymization techniques to protect user privacy.

- **User-Controlled Data:** Emerging regulations and technologies will empower individuals to control how their data is collected, used, and shared.

12.4.2 Cloud and Hybrid Security

- **Cloud-Centric Strategies:** As businesses migrate to cloud services, securing these environments will become a top priority. This includes developing robust identity and access management (IAM) systems and securing APIs.

- **Hybrid Models:** Organizations will need to balance on-premise and cloud-based security measures to protect data across diverse environments.

12.4.3 Convergence of IT and Operational Technology (OT) Security

- **Unified Security Frameworks:** The convergence of IT and OT systems—especially in critical infrastructure—requires integrated security strategies that cover both domains.

- **Industrial IoT (IIoT) Challenges:** Securing the IIoT will be paramount as industrial networks become increasingly interconnected and vulnerable to cyber threats.

12.5 Preparing the Cybersecurity Workforce for the Future

The rapid evolution of cybersecurity technology and threats demands a workforce that is skilled, agile, and continuously learning. This section discusses the future of cybersecurity careers:

12.5.1 Emphasizing Continuous Education and Training

- **Ongoing Learning:** Professionals will need to stay updated with emerging technologies and threat landscapes through certifications, courses, and real-world training.

- **Cross-Disciplinary Skills:** The integration of AI, quantum computing, and blockchain into cybersecurity requires knowledge that spans multiple disciplines.

12.5.2 Addressing the Talent Shortage

- **Diversity and Inclusion:** Encouraging a diverse range of perspectives and backgrounds will be critical in building a robust cybersecurity workforce.

- **Automation and Augmentation:** While automation can handle routine tasks, human expertise is still essential for strategic decision-making and threat analysis.

12.6 Strategies to Future-Proof Your Cybersecurity Posture

Preparing for the future involves proactive measures and strategic planning. Here are some key strategies:

12.6.1 Embrace a Culture of Continuous Improvement

- **Regular Audits and Reviews:** Continuously assess and update security policies and technologies to adapt to emerging threats.

- **Scenario Planning:** Conduct regular simulations and tabletop exercises to test and refine your incident response plans.

12.6.2 Invest in Next-Generation Technologies

- **Pilot Programs:** Implement pilot projects to explore the benefits of AI-driven security, blockchain applications, and quantum-resistant encryption.

- **Collaborative Partnerships:** Work with technology providers, research institutions, and industry consortia to stay at the forefront of cybersecurity innovation.

12.6.3 Adopt Adaptive Security Frameworks

- **Zero Trust Implementation:** Transition to a zero trust architecture that continuously validates every access attempt.

- **Security Automation:** Leverage automation to improve detection, response times, and overall efficiency in managing threats.

12.7 Conclusion

The future of cybersecurity is shaped by rapid technological advancements, emerging threats, and the continuous evolution of defense strategies. In this chapter, we have explored:

- **Emerging Threats:** The rise of AI-powered attacks, quantum computing challenges, and vulnerabilities in IoT and supply chains.

- **Innovative Technologies:** How AI, quantum-safe cryptography, blockchain, and zero trust models are revolutionizing cybersecurity practices.

- **Future Trends:** The growing focus on privacy, the convergence of cloud and hybrid security, and the integration of IT and OT systems.

- **Workforce Evolution:** The importance of continuous education, cross-disciplinary skills, and addressing the cybersecurity talent shortage.

- **Strategic Preparedness:** Practical strategies to future-proof your cybersecurity posture through adaptive frameworks, continuous improvement, and proactive investments.

By staying informed about these trends and technologies, you can position yourself and your organization to better anticipate and counter future threats. The landscape of cybersecurity will undoubtedly continue to evolve, but with a commitment to innovation, continuous learning, and adaptive strategies, you can build a resilient defense that stands the test of time.

As we move forward, the next chapter will provide a comprehensive list of resources, tools, and additional reading to further empower you on your journey toward a safer digital life.

Chapter 13: Resources and Tools for Continued Protection

Cybersecurity is not a one-and-done task—it requires ongoing vigilance, continuous learning, and the regular adoption of new tools and practices. In this chapter, we provide a comprehensive list of resources and tools that can help you maintain and enhance your cybersecurity posture over time. Whether you're an individual seeking to secure your personal digital life or a small business owner striving to safeguard your operations, these resources will serve as a roadmap for continued protection.

13.1 Introduction

In today's rapidly evolving digital landscape, staying informed and equipped with the latest cybersecurity tools is essential. This chapter is designed to guide you through:

- **Essential Tools and Software:** A curated list of must-have applications and services for protection.

- **Educational Resources:** Courses, certifications, and reading materials to deepen your understanding of cybersecurity.

- **Community and Professional Networks:** Forums and groups that provide peer support, industry news, and expert advice.

- **Personalized Cybersecurity Planning:** Steps to create and maintain a long-term security strategy tailored to your needs.

By leveraging these resources, you can keep pace with emerging threats and continuously improve your defense mechanisms.

13.2 Essential Cybersecurity Tools

A robust cybersecurity strategy is built on a strong foundation of software and hardware tools. Consider integrating the following into your routine:

13.2.1 Antivirus and Anti-Malware Software

- **Reputable Solutions:** Software like Bitdefender, Norton, Kaspersky, and Malwarebytes offer real-time protection against viruses, ransomware, and spyware.

- **Regular Scanning:** Ensure your chosen software provides scheduled scans and automatic updates to catch new threats promptly.

13.2.2 Firewalls and Intrusion Detection Systems (IDS/IPS)

- **Hardware Firewalls:** Many modern routers come with built-in firewalls; consider upgrading to models with advanced security features.

- **Software Firewalls:** Use operating system–integrated firewalls or third-party applications for an added layer of defense.

- **IDS/IPS Tools:** For advanced users or small businesses, tools like Snort or OSSEC help monitor network traffic and detect intrusions.

13.2.3 Virtual Private Networks (VPNs)

- **Trusted Providers:** Services such as NordVPN, ExpressVPN, and ProtonVPN encrypt your internet traffic, especially important on public Wi-Fi networks.

- **Privacy Protection:** A VPN masks your IP address and helps prevent tracking by third parties.

13.2.4 Password Managers

- **Secure Storage:** Applications like LastPass, 1Password, and Bitwarden generate, store, and manage unique, complex passwords for all your accounts.

- **Ease of Use:** These tools help you avoid password reuse and simplify the process of maintaining strong credentials.

13.2.5 Encryption Tools

- **Full-Disk Encryption:** Utilize built-in tools like BitLocker (Windows) or FileVault (macOS) to secure your device's data.

- **File Encryption:** Tools such as VeraCrypt or AxCrypt can encrypt sensitive files before sharing or storing them.

13.3 Recommended Software and Applications

In addition to the core tools, several specialized applications can further enhance your cybersecurity:

- **Secure Browsers:** Use privacy-focused browsers like Mozilla Firefox or Brave, which offer enhanced tracking protection and regular security updates.

- **Ad and Tracker Blockers:** Extensions such as uBlock Origin, Privacy Badger, or Ghostery help prevent tracking and reduce exposure to malvertising.

- **Email Security Tools:** Consider using encrypted email services like ProtonMail or Tutanota, and install spam filters to minimize phishing risks.

- **Backup Solutions:** Employ cloud services with robust encryption (e.g., Backblaze, Carbonite) or set up regular local backups to secure critical data.

13.4 Cybersecurity Communities and Professional Networks

Staying connected with like-minded professionals and enthusiasts is invaluable for continuous learning and support:

13.4.1 Online Forums and Discussion Groups

- **Reddit:** Subreddits such as r/cybersecurity, r/netsec, and r/privacy provide insights, news, and peer support.

- **Stack Exchange:** The Information Security Stack Exchange offers expert Q&A on a wide range of cybersecurity topics.

- **Specialized Forums:** Websites like BleepingComputer and Wilders Security Forums host active communities for technical support and discussion.

13.4.2 Industry Organizations and Conferences

- **Professional Groups:** Organizations such as (ISC)², ISACA, and CompTIA offer resources, certifications, and networking opportunities.

- **Conferences and Webinars:** Attend events like DEF CON, Black Hat, RSA Conference, or regional cybersecurity meetups to stay updated on the latest trends and solutions.

13.5 Continuing Education and Certifications

Cybersecurity is a rapidly evolving field. Ongoing education is key to staying ahead of threats:

13.5.1 Online Courses and Training Platforms

- **MOOCs and e-Learning:** Platforms like Coursera, Udemy, Cybrary, and edX offer courses ranging from beginner to advanced cybersecurity topics.

- **Vendor-Specific Training:** Many cybersecurity vendors provide free or paid training on their products, which can be invaluable for both personal and professional growth.

13.5.2 Certifications to Consider

- **Entry-Level Certifications:** CompTIA Security+ provides a solid foundation for understanding cybersecurity principles.

- **Advanced Certifications:** Consider pursuing certifications like Certified Information Systems Security Professional (CISSP), Certified Ethical Hacker (CEH), or Certified Information Security Manager (CISM) as you advance.

- **Specialized Training:** Explore niche certifications in areas such as cloud security, penetration testing, or incident response to deepen your expertise.

13.6 Additional Reading and Cybersecurity News

Staying informed through reputable sources is crucial:

13.6.1 Blogs and Websites

- **Krebs on Security:** Brian Krebs' blog offers in-depth analysis and investigative reporting on cybersecurity incidents.

- **The Hacker News:** A widely followed source for the latest cybersecurity news, trends, and threat alerts.

- **Dark Reading:** Provides a comprehensive overview of the cybersecurity industry, including research, news, and expert opinions.

13.6.2 Government and Industry Reports

- **US-CERT and NIST:** Regular publications and alerts from the United States Computer Emergency Readiness Team and the National Institute of Standards and Technology provide guidance and updates on vulnerabilities and best practices.

- **Annual Reports:** Review reports from cybersecurity firms (e.g., Verizon's Data Breach Investigations Report, Symantec's Internet Security Threat Report) to understand broader trends and emerging threats.

13.7 Creating a Personalized Cybersecurity Action Plan

A one-size-fits-all approach does not work in cybersecurity. Tailor your defenses by creating a personalized action plan:

13.7.1 Assessing Your Needs and Risks

- **Conduct a Self-Audit:** Identify the devices, data, and online accounts that require protection.

- **Prioritize Vulnerabilities:** Evaluate which areas present the greatest risk and need immediate attention.

13.7.2 Setting Goals and Milestones

- **Short-Term Goals:** Implement basic security measures such as enabling two-factor authentication, updating software, and installing a reputable antivirus.

- **Long-Term Strategies:** Plan for regular training, periodic security audits, and the adoption of emerging technologies as your needs evolve.

13.7.3 Documenting and Reviewing Your Plan

- **Action Checklist:** Create a checklist of security tasks to be reviewed and updated monthly or quarterly.

- **Feedback and Adaptation:** Monitor the effectiveness of your measures, gather feedback from trusted sources, and adjust your plan as new threats emerge.

13.8 Conclusion

Continued protection in an ever-changing digital world requires a proactive, informed, and adaptive approach. In this chapter, you have learned:

- **The Importance of Essential Tools:** From antivirus software to password managers and VPNs, robust tools form the backbone of effective cybersecurity.

- **Recommended Software and Applications:** Additional applications can further shield you from evolving threats.

- **The Value of Community and Continuous Education:** Staying connected with professional networks and pursuing ongoing education and certifications is key to long-term success.

- **Personalized Cybersecurity Planning:** Developing and regularly updating your cybersecurity action plan ensures that your defenses evolve with the threat landscape.

By integrating these resources and strategies into your routine, you will be well-prepared to face the challenges of tomorrow's digital environment. The next chapter will wrap up this guide by summarizing key takeaways and empowering you to take charge of your cybersecurity journey.

Chapter 14: Conclusion: Empowering Yourself in a Connected World

As our journey through the realm of cybersecurity comes to a close, this final chapter brings together the key insights, practical strategies, and motivational messages presented throughout the guide. In today's increasingly interconnected digital world, empowering yourself to protect your online presence is not merely a technical necessity—it is a fundamental aspect of preserving your personal privacy, financial security, and overall well-being. This chapter summarizes the core concepts, reinforces the importance of continuous vigilance, and inspires you to take decisive action in safeguarding your digital life.

14.1 Recap of Key Takeaways

14.1.1 Understanding the Digital Landscape

- **The Evolution of Technology:** We have witnessed a transformation from basic online interactions to a complex ecosystem of interconnected devices, cloud services, and IoT technologies. With each advancement, new opportunities and risks emerge.

- **The Dual Nature of Connectivity:** While digital connectivity brings unparalleled convenience and access to information, it also opens the door to sophisticated cyber threats that target individuals, businesses, and communities.

14.1.2 Grasping Core Cybersecurity Concepts

- **Foundational Knowledge:** From encryption and firewalls to multi-factor authentication and zero trust models, understanding these concepts equips you with the language and tools to navigate the cybersecurity landscape.

- **Practical Application:** Emphasis was placed on translating complex ideas into everyday practices—whether through safe browsing, device security, or strong password management—that empower you to implement robust security measures.

14.1.3 Implementing a Multi-Layered Defense

- **Holistic Protection:** Cybersecurity is most effective when it combines technical safeguards (like antivirus software, VPNs, and encryption) with proactive behavioral practices (such as vigilant online habits and regular software updates).

- **Personal and Business Strategies:** Whether you are an individual protecting your personal data or a small business owner safeguarding company assets, layered defenses and continuous improvement are key to mitigating risks.

14.1.4 Responding and Adapting to Cyber Incidents

- **Incident Response:** A well-prepared response plan, including detection, containment, eradication, and recovery procedures, is crucial for minimizing damage when a breach occurs.

- **Learning and Evolving:** Every incident offers lessons that help refine your security strategy. Continuous education, regular audits, and scenario planning are essential for staying ahead of emerging threats.

14.1.5 Looking Toward the Future

- **Emerging Trends:** The future of cybersecurity will be shaped by advancements in artificial intelligence, quantum computing, blockchain, and other disruptive technologies. Staying informed and adaptable is crucial.

- **Empowerment through Resources:** Leveraging the extensive resources, communities, and tools discussed in this guide will enable you to continuously protect and enhance your digital security.

14.2 Building a Cybersecurity Mindset

14.2.1 Proactive Vigilance

- **Continuous Learning:** Cyber threats evolve rapidly; make a commitment to ongoing education through courses, webinars, and industry news.

- **Risk Awareness:** Cultivate a mindset that is always alert to potential vulnerabilities—both technical and behavioral—in your digital interactions.

14.2.2 Personal Responsibility and Empowerment

- **Taking Charge:** Whether it's updating your software, managing your passwords, or adjusting your privacy settings, every small step contributes to a larger shield of protection.

- **Empowering Others:** Share your knowledge with family, friends, and colleagues. Encourage a community-wide commitment to cybersecurity best practices.

14.2.3 Embracing Adaptability

- **Dynamic Defense:** Understand that cybersecurity is not a one-time setup but a continuous process of adaptation. Regularly revisit your security practices and make necessary adjustments.

- **Resilience Through Innovation:** Keep an open mind to emerging technologies and strategies that can further fortify your defenses against future threats.

14.3 Action Steps for a Safer Digital Life

14.3.1 Immediate Actions

- **Audit Your Digital Presence:** Conduct a thorough review of your devices, online accounts, and connected services to identify potential vulnerabilities.

- **Strengthen Your Defenses:** Implement or update key security measures—such as enabling multi-factor authentication, updating software, and using a reputable password manager.

- **Backup Your Data:** Ensure that all important data is regularly backed up in a secure and encrypted manner.

14.3.2 Medium-Term Strategies

- **Develop a Cybersecurity Plan:** Create a personalized action plan that outlines specific security goals and tasks, complete with regular review intervals.

- **Educate Yourself and Others:** Invest time in learning more about cybersecurity trends and share that knowledge within your personal and professional networks.

- **Monitor Your Security:** Utilize the tools and resources provided—like VPNs, antivirus programs, and security audits—to maintain continuous oversight of your digital environment.

14.3.3 Long-Term Commitment

- **Stay Informed:** Subscribe to reputable cybersecurity blogs, newsletters, and professional forums to stay updated on the latest developments.

- **Plan for the Future:** Regularly update your incident response and business continuity plans to accommodate emerging threats and technologies.

- **Advocate for Security:** Support initiatives and policies that promote stronger cybersecurity practices both locally and globally.

14.4 Final Thoughts: Your Role in a Connected World

The digital era has transformed the way we live, work, and interact. With this transformation comes both immense opportunity and significant responsibility. Cybersecurity is not solely the domain of IT professionals—it is a shared responsibility that impacts every individual and organization. By applying the knowledge and strategies outlined in this guide, you are taking crucial steps toward protecting not only your digital life but also contributing to a safer, more secure digital community.

Empowerment in the connected world means being proactive, informed, and resilient in the face of evolving cyber threats. As you continue your journey, remember that every measure you take enhances your security and strengthens the collective defense against cybercrime.

14.5 Conclusion

In summary, this guide has provided you with:

- **A comprehensive understanding** of the digital landscape and the myriad cyber threats that exist.

- **Practical, actionable strategies** to secure your devices, manage your data, and safeguard your digital identity.

- **A roadmap for continuous improvement,** leveraging both current tools and emerging technologies to build a resilient cybersecurity posture.

- **Inspiration and empowerment** to take control of your online security and foster a culture of vigilance among your peers.

The future of cybersecurity is a collaborative endeavor. As you implement these practices, share your experiences and insights with your community, and remain adaptable to change, you will not only protect yourself but also help shape a more secure digital environment for everyone.

Take charge of your cybersecurity journey today, and step confidently into a connected world where your digital freedom and privacy are safeguarded by your informed, proactive actions.

Embrace the challenge, stay curious, and let your commitment to cybersecurity empower you—and those around you—to thrive in the digital age.

Appendix A: Glossary of Cybersecurity Terms

This appendix provides a comprehensive glossary of key cybersecurity terms and acronyms used throughout the guide. Whether you're new to the subject or looking for a quick refresher, this glossary is designed to clarify essential concepts and technologies that underpin modern cybersecurity practices.

A.1 Access and Authentication

Access Control

The process of regulating who or what can view or use resources in a computing environment. Access control mechanisms ensure that only authorized users or devices can access specific data, systems, or networks.

Authentication

The verification process used to confirm a user's, device's, or entity's identity before granting access to resources. Methods include passwords, biometrics, and multi-factor authentication.

Multi-Factor Authentication (MFA)

A security approach that requires users to provide two or more verification factors (something you know, something you have, or something you are) to gain access. This adds additional layers of protection beyond just a username and password.

Biometric Authentication

A type of authentication that uses unique biological characteristics, such as fingerprints, facial recognition, or retinal scans, to verify a user's identity.

A.2 Data Protection and Encryption

Backup

The process of copying and archiving data to ensure its availability in the event of data loss, corruption, or a cybersecurity incident. Backups can be stored on external drives, cloud services, or other secure locations.

Encryption

The conversion of data into a coded form to prevent unauthorized access. Encryption ensures that even if data is intercepted, it remains unreadable without the proper decryption key.

Full-Disk Encryption

A method of encryption that protects all data stored on a device's hard drive, ensuring that unauthorized users cannot access the information even if they have physical possession of the device.

A.3 Network and Perimeter Security

Firewall

A network security system that monitors and controls incoming and outgoing network traffic based on predetermined security rules. Firewalls can be hardware-based, software-based, or a combination of both, acting as a barrier between trusted and untrusted networks.

Virtual Private Network (VPN)

A service that creates a secure, encrypted connection over a public or shared network. VPNs are used to protect online privacy by masking IP addresses and encrypting data transmitted between the user's device and the internet.

Intrusion Detection System (IDS)

A system that monitors network or system activities for malicious activities or policy violations. IDS tools analyze traffic patterns and generate alerts when suspicious activity is detected.

Intrusion Prevention System (IPS)

Similar to an IDS, but with the additional capability of taking automatic action—such as blocking traffic—to prevent detected threats from causing harm.

A.4 Threats and Attack Techniques

Malware
A general term for malicious software designed to harm, exploit, or otherwise compromise devices, networks, or data. This includes viruses, worms, trojans, spyware, and ransomware.

Ransomware
A type of malware that encrypts a victim's files or locks their device, then demands payment (often in cryptocurrency) to restore access.

Phishing
A social engineering attack where cybercriminals send fraudulent communications—often via email or SMS—that appear to come from reputable sources, with the goal of tricking individuals into revealing sensitive information such as login credentials or financial details.

Smishing
A form of phishing conducted via SMS text messages, aimed at luring individuals into divulging personal or financial information or installing malicious software.

Social Engineering
The art of manipulating people into performing actions or divulging confidential information. Tactics can include impersonation, urgency, or other psychological techniques to bypass security controls.

Advanced Persistent Threat (APT)

A prolonged and targeted cyberattack in which an intruder gains access to a network and remains undetected for an extended period. APTs are typically aimed at large organizations or nation-states to steal sensitive data or disrupt operations.

Deepfake

Media (video, audio, or images) created or altered using advanced artificial intelligence techniques to convincingly impersonate a real person. Deepfakes can be used in cyberattacks to manipulate perceptions or execute sophisticated scams.

A.5 Emerging Technologies and Security Models

Artificial Intelligence (AI) and Machine Learning (ML)

Technologies that enable computers to learn from data and make decisions with minimal human intervention. In cybersecurity, AI and ML are used to detect anomalies, identify threats, and automate responses to security incidents.

Quantum Computing

A form of computing that leverages quantum-mechanical phenomena to perform calculations at speeds unattainable by classical computers. While promising for many fields, quantum computing poses a potential risk to traditional encryption methods.

Quantum-Safe Cryptography

New cryptographic algorithms being developed to secure data against the potential threats posed by quantum computers. These algorithms are designed to be resistant to attacks that exploit quantum computing power.

Blockchain

A decentralized, distributed ledger technology that records transactions across many computers so that the records cannot be altered retroactively. In cybersecurity, blockchain can be used for secure data sharing, identity verification, and ensuring data integrity.

Zero Trust Architecture

A security model that assumes no implicit trust for any user, device, or application, whether inside or outside the network. Every access request must be thoroughly verified, and access is granted on a least-privilege basis.

A.6 Additional Terms

Digital Footprint

The trail of data left behind by an individual's online activities, including posts, browsing history, and interactions on social media. Managing one's digital footprint is crucial for protecting privacy and reputation.

Incident Response

The process and procedures implemented to detect, respond to, and recover from cybersecurity incidents.

Effective incident response minimizes damage and helps prevent future breaches.

Security Information and Event Management (SIEM)

Systems that aggregate and analyze activity from multiple resources across an organization's IT infrastructure. SIEM solutions help in real-time threat detection, compliance, and incident management.

Honeypot

A security mechanism that creates a decoy system to attract cyberattacks. By studying the attackers' methods, honeypots provide valuable insights into threat behavior and vulnerabilities.

A.7 Acronyms

- **APT:** Advanced Persistent Threat
- **MFA:** Multi-Factor Authentication
- **IDS:** Intrusion Detection System
- **IPS:** Intrusion Prevention System
- **VPN:** Virtual Private Network
- **AI:** Artificial Intelligence
- **ML:** Machine Learning
- **SIEM:** Security Information and Event Management
- **IoT:** Internet of Things

This glossary is intended as a reference tool to help you better understand the terminology used in cybersecurity. Familiarity with these terms will enhance your ability to navigate the digital security landscape, interpret best practices, and engage with more advanced materials as you continue your cybersecurity journey.

Appendix B: Cybersecurity Action Plans and Checklists

This appendix is designed to serve as a practical companion to the main guide. It offers actionable templates, checklists, and sample plans that you can customize to suit your personal or organizational cybersecurity needs. Whether you're looking to assess your current security posture, develop an incident response strategy, or establish ongoing maintenance practices, these tools will help you implement and maintain robust cybersecurity defenses.

B.1 Introduction

Cybersecurity is an ongoing process that requires planning, regular evaluation, and prompt action. In this appendix, you will find:

- **Self-Assessment Checklists:** To help you evaluate your current security measures.

- **Incident Response Checklists:** To guide you through immediate actions when a security incident occurs.

- **Action Plan Templates:** To create and implement policies, training, and maintenance schedules.

- **Audit and Maintenance Schedules:** To ensure continuous improvement and adaptation to new threats.

Use these resources as a starting point, and tailor them to your specific environment—whether that's your personal digital life or the security strategy of a small business.

B.2 Cybersecurity Self-Assessment Checklist

Regular self-assessments are crucial to identify vulnerabilities and measure the effectiveness of your cybersecurity measures. Consider using the following checklist periodically:

Asset Identification

- **Inventory of Devices:** List all computers, mobile devices, IoT devices, and other hardware.

- **Software and Applications:** Catalog all installed software, including operating systems, applications, and security tools.

- **Data Assets:** Identify sensitive data repositories, such as financial records, personal documents, and proprietary business information.

Vulnerability and Risk Evaluation

- **Software Updates:** Verify that all devices and applications have the latest updates and security patches installed.

- **Password Practices:** Review password strength and uniqueness for all accounts; ensure the use of a password manager.

- **Access Controls:** Check that access to systems and data is restricted based on roles and that multi-factor authentication is enabled where available.

- **Backup Procedures:** Confirm that data backups are being performed regularly and stored securely.

Security Tools and Configurations

- **Antivirus/Anti-Malware:** Ensure that reputable security software is installed and functioning.

- **Firewalls and VPNs:** Verify that firewalls are active on devices and routers, and that VPNs are used on unsecured networks.

- **Encryption:** Check that sensitive data is encrypted both in transit and at rest.

- **Network Monitoring:** Confirm that intrusion detection/prevention systems (IDS/IPS) and logging mechanisms are operational.

B.3 Incident Response Checklist

A swift and organized response is essential when a cyber incident occurs. Use this checklist to ensure no critical step is overlooked:

Immediate Actions

- **Detection:** Identify and verify signs of a potential security breach or suspicious activity.

- **Containment:** Isolate affected systems from the network to prevent further spread.

- **Notification:** Alert the designated incident response team or IT personnel.

- **Documentation:** Begin a detailed log of the incident, including date, time, affected systems, and observed behavior.

Investigation and Eradication

- **Forensic Analysis:** Collect and preserve evidence from affected systems (logs, files, network traffic).

- **Threat Removal:** Use antivirus and malware removal tools to eradicate identified threats.

- **Patch Vulnerabilities:** Identify and apply patches or configuration changes to eliminate vulnerabilities exploited by the attackers.

- **Credential Resets:** Change passwords and update

authentication methods for compromised accounts.

Recovery and Post-Incident Review

- **System Restoration:** Restore systems from clean backups and verify integrity.

- **Testing:** Conduct thorough testing to ensure all systems are secure and functioning correctly.

- **Communication:** Notify stakeholders and, if required, report the incident to regulatory bodies.

- **Post-Incident Analysis:** Conduct a debriefing to identify lessons learned and update policies and procedures accordingly.

B.4 Cybersecurity Policy and Action Plan Template

Establishing a formal cybersecurity policy is critical for both personal and organizational security. Use this template as a framework:

Policy Statement

- **Objective:** Define the purpose and scope of your cybersecurity policy.

- **Applicability:** Identify the devices, systems, and data covered under the policy.

- **Responsibilities:** Specify roles for employees, IT staff, and management regarding cybersecurity.

Key Components

- **Access Control:** Outline guidelines for user authentication, account management, and access restrictions.

- **Data Protection:** Define protocols for data encryption, storage, backup, and secure disposal.

- **Incident Response:** Provide a clear incident response plan, including roles, reporting procedures, and escalation processes.

- **Training and Awareness:** Establish a schedule for regular cybersecurity training and updates for all stakeholders.

- **Compliance and Auditing:** Set standards for compliance with relevant laws and regulations, and plan regular security audits.

Implementation Timeline

- **Immediate (0-3 Months):** Update software, enforce strong password policies, and implement basic security tools.

- **Short-Term (3-6 Months):** Roll out cybersecurity training, complete a comprehensive self-assessment, and update incident response plans.

- **Long-Term (6-12 Months):** Review and refine policies, conduct periodic audits, and integrate advanced security measures as needed.

B.5 Regular Maintenance and Audit Schedule

Continuous monitoring and regular maintenance are key to sustaining cybersecurity over time. Consider the following schedule:

Daily

- Check system alerts and logs for unusual activity.

- Verify that antivirus and firewall systems are active.

Weekly

- Perform routine scans for malware and vulnerabilities.

- Review user account activity and access logs.

Monthly

- Update all software, including operating systems and applications.

- Back up critical data and test restoration procedures.

- Audit connected devices and review network configurations.

Quarterly

- Conduct a comprehensive cybersecurity self-assessment using the provided checklist.

- Update incident response plans based on new threats or lessons learned.

- Hold a cybersecurity training refresher for all users.

Annually

- Review and update the overall cybersecurity policy.

- Schedule a full external security audit or penetration test.

- Reassess technology investments and plan for future security enhancements.

B.6 Additional Resources for Implementation

To further support your cybersecurity initiatives, consider the following types of resources:

- **Templates and Tools:** Look for free and paid cybersecurity policy templates, checklists, and audit tools available from reputable cybersecurity organizations.

- **Consulting Services:** Engage with cybersecurity experts or managed service providers for tailored advice and assistance.

- **Training Programs:** Invest in online courses and certification programs to deepen your cybersecurity knowledge and skills.

- **Industry Reports:** Regularly review reports from organizations like NIST, Verizon, and cybersecurity research firms to stay informed on emerging threats and best practices.

B.7 Conclusion

This appendix is intended to empower you to take actionable steps toward a stronger cybersecurity posture. By using the checklists, templates, and schedules provided here, you can:

- **Assess** your current security measures.

- **Plan** and **implement** robust cybersecurity policies.

- **Respond** swiftly and effectively to incidents.

- **Maintain** a culture of continuous improvement.

Regularly revisiting and updating these plans will ensure that you remain prepared for evolving cyber threats and can confidently navigate the digital landscape. Use these tools as a foundation for ongoing protection, and customize them to meet the unique needs of your personal or organizational environment.

With Appendix B, you now have a practical toolkit to complement the conceptual knowledge provided in the main guide. Empower yourself to take control of your digital security and build a resilient, proactive defense against cyber threats.

www.ingramcontent.com/pod-product-compliance
Lightning Source LLC
LaVergne TN
LVHW021459170326
834004LV00004B/350